The Stray Branch

Fall/Winter 2013

Cover Art "X Ray" Rex Sexton

The Stray Branch
Fall/Winter 2013 #12 Vol 9
© 2013 The Stray Branch. All Rights Reserved.
Contributors retain all copyrights to their work.

Rex Sexton is a Surrealist painter based in Philadelphia and Chicago. His award winning art has been televised on PBS, written about in newspapers, reproduced in magazines and included in national and international exhibitions. Of his recent exhibit in Chicago the critique Robin Dulzen wrote in Chicago Art Magazine: "Sexton's work ... brings to mind the flattened forms and spaces and line qualities of Miro ... {and} the bizarre figures and spaces of Chagall. Bridging reality and fantasy, Sexton's paintings emotionally engage viewers with multitudes of figures and multitudes of vivid expressions." Jeffery McNary wrote in New City: "Growing up in Chicago's Back of the Yards neighborhood, Sexton 'saw hardships with no let up.' He paints 'expressions of humanity with the hope that I capture its dreams in the midst of adversity."

"Romanticism emerges in his stunning "Edith" oil painting. This semi-cubist portrait of Edith Piaf seduces with thick, deep layers of tans and blacks, doe eyes and arched eyebrows."

thestraybranch.org
thestraybranchlitmag@yahoo.com
Founded/Edited by Debbie Berk
Prepared for publication by Debbie Berk

Printed in the U.S.A.

ISBN-13: 978-0615880525 (The Stray Branch)

ISBN-10: 0615880525

Editor's Notes

Welcome to the Fall/Winter 2013 issue. Submissions resume October 1st. Submission needs are for art and photography for the #13, Spring/Summer 2014 issue and #14 the Fall/Winter 2014 issue. All art and photography will be considered for the covers of these issues. Due to my on going backlog all poetry and fiction will be considered for the Spring/Summer 2015 issue.

Guidelines for art and photography: Looking for dark, gothic, edgy, odd, haunting, surreal, emotional, reflective and unique work. Complete guidelines for all submissions can be found on the website.

Sincerely,

Debbie Berk

Debbie Berk
Founder/Editor
The Stray Branch
http://www.thestraybranch.org
thestraybranchlitmag@yahoo.com

Acknowledgements:

Il Connoisseur Sanguinante by Matt Dennison
(published in The Spoon River Poetry Review, 2007)

Post Card by John T. Hitchner *previously published online*

Featured......

All contributors, poems, fiction, art and photography chosen as features also appears on the website

Featured Poems:

Unaligned. In a Forgotten Wind. by A. J. Huffman ....pg 76
Confessional by Brendan Sullivan ....pg 53
Bird by Ivy Page ....pg 45
Out With The Girls by John David Muth ....pg 72
Driving Into November by John T. Hitchner ....pg 78
Even At The End by Matthew Rodgers ....pg 50
Egyptian Night by Roger Singer ....pg 70
They Sent Him For Pills by Timothy B. Dodd ....pg 66
Morning's Choice by Valentina Cano ....pg 68
No Control by Elizabeth Swados ....pg 51

Featured Fiction:

The Swarm by Mark Slade ....pg 33-34
Hands by Terence Kuch ....pg 62-63
In The Night Kitchen by Simone Martel ....pg 1-3

Featured Artist:

Amanda Turco ....pg 23-29

Featured Contributors:

Annie Neugebauer
Poet / pg 30-31

Mark Burchard
Poet & Photographer
pg / 8-16

Michael Mc Aloran
Poet / pg 6-7

Bruce D. Millar
Poet / pg 64-65

G. David Schwartz
Poet / pg 101-102

Philip Tinkler
Poet / pg 37

The Stray Branch
Fall/Winter
#12 Vol 9

www.thestraybranch.org
thestraybranchlitmag@yahoo.com

Founder/Editor Debbie Berk

Contents:

Poets/Poetry

A.J. Huffman
Unaligned. In a Forgotten Wind. / 76
Implosion / 76
Dancing in the Temple of Hell / 76

Amber Koneval
Blood Splatterpaint / 38

Annie Neugebauer
Deceptive Passages / 31
Get Over / 30
Anxiety / 32

ayaz daryl nielsen
dragonfly / 54
verdict / 54

Brendan Sullivan
Torn / 52
Serial Boy / 52
Confessional / 53
Wires / 53

Bruce Millar
Those Drinking Days / 64-65

Catfish McDaris
Climbing Icicles / 93

Dana Stamps, ll
My Dad's Way / 100

Daniel J. Langton
Again   This   Evening / 90

David Lawrence
Spooning / 67
Endless Passage / 67
Green House / 67

Denny Marshall
Space Dreams / 94
S Mail received / 94

Elizabeth Swados
No Control / 51

Erren Geraud Kelly
Joshua (aubade) / 10

Frank De Canio
Shifty as Charged / 85
Clockwise / 85

Frank S. LeRose
In Gray Days / 5
Servants of Disgrace / 5
Trichioroethane / 5

G. David Schwartz
They Hit Me Like A Pillow / 102
Without Wings Made Me Tear / 101

Ivy Page
Girl / 43
At 14 / 44
Bird / 45
To Bring Me Home / 43
Hand / 45

James Dye
View of Taunt / 97
Meaningless Heart / 97

Jay Dardes
Omen / 99
Pat / 99

John David Muth
Supper Alone / 73
Out With The Girls / 72

John T. Hitchner
Post Card / 77
Driving Into November / 78
Pieces of a Life Between Lattitudes / 79
Last Shot / 80
Old Friends Then and Now / 81

j.p.christiansen
Somewhere In The Night. / 82
Refugee. / 83 - 84
Tomorrow Is Another Day. / 84

Krikor Der Hohannesian
A Way of Life / 91
What Do You Do? / 92

Poets/Poetry Continued

Mark Burchard
    After Midnight / 10-16
    Free / 8
    On Leaving / 9

Martin Willitts Jr.
    Why Can't I Remember / 74
    Reaching Us / 75
    Letting Anger Go / 75

Matt Dennison
    11 Connoisseur Sanguinante / 35

Matthew Raynor
    HEARTACHE IS A LONER / 71

Matthew Rodgers
    Even At The End / 50

Michael Lee Johnson
    I Know From My Bed / 19
    Cold Gray / 17
    Even as Evening / 18

Michael M. Marks
    Meteorror Horror / 36

Michael Mc Aloran
    #9 - / 6
    #11 - / 6
    #14 - / 7
    #15 - / 7
    #16 - / 7
    #25 - / 7

Patrick Sugrue
    Poor Cousin Ed / 98

Paul David Adkins
    Mrs. Savoy Makes The Brushes / 22

Peter J. Grieco
    REVERIES / 48
    OTOPATHY / 49

Philip Tinkler
    PSEUDOCIDE IN CLUB 27 / 37

Robert E. Petras
    GRAY WINDOW / 4

Roger Singer
    EGYPTIAN NIGHT / 70

Sarah Anne Stinnett
    The Broken Era / 46
    Things I Didn't Know I Love / 47

Simon Perchik
    1 / 95
    3 / 96

Timothy B. Dodd
    They Sent Him For Pills / 66

Valentina Cano
    A Drowning / 68
    First Day of Summer / 69
    Morning's Choice / 68

Fiction

Body Bag by Eric Bonholtzer / 55-61
Tuesday Night Bowling by Lily Murphy / 20-21
The Swarm by Mark Slade / 33-34
Far From It by Ron Koppelberger / 88-89
The Pumpkin by Ron Koppelberger / 87
In The Night Kitchen by Simone Martel / 1-3
Hands by Terence Kuch / 62-63

Action Spurs Creativity
    A dark commentary by Shane Armstrong / 39-41

Artwork

Amanda Turco
    A Love Beyond / 24
    Burden of Responibility / 25
    Chickadee / 26
    Daemon / 27
    Hearts War / 23
    Jack / 28
    Loss of Innocents / 29

Rex Sexton
    Echoes in the Attic / 94
    Eye Spy / 42
    Talking Heads / 99
    Witch / 86

Photography

Mark Burchard / 10 -16
Sally Burnette / 53

Cover art X-Ray Eyes by Rex Sexton

~ ~ ~

In the Night Kitchen
Fiction by Simone Martel

4am. Face in pillow. Arm flails. Hand hits cat. Snarl, bite.

Raise my face. Light under the door. Pull sweats on over nakedness. Follow light to kitchen. Son looks up from computer, flinches.

Your face looks dragged down.

I used to walk into a restaurant knowing I was the prettiest woman there. Best legs, arms, hair, best face.

Go away, Mom. I'm staying up till I reach the next level.

How do I connect with my son? At his age I went for long walks with my Dad. Okay, partly for weight management. But we walked fast, after dinner, before homework, talked about existentialism, meaning/meaninglessness of life. I don't think my son cares about that shit. At least he doesn't talk to me about it.   Would a daughter?

Your face looks dragged down. Looking up from his computer with disgust.

Imagine a daughter knocking on my bedroom door, later. Mom? I'm sorry.

Son just sleeps. Sleep of the innocent. Men.

Walking with my dad, our long strides striking out. You remind me of a young Kate Hepburn. How much do you weigh?

116.

Never weigh more than that.

Well, Dad, I do. Do you still love me?

In the kitchen, quarter past 4, I squirt red wine from a box into a mug. I've started ordering white when I go out, started associating red with pain.
Back to bed, briefly, with the mug.

116, in my skin tight jeans.

Bouncing up again, off the mattress. Not quite tipsy. Walk into kitchen, toward the light, in my pulled-on soft clothes. Son's fingers rattling on the keyboard, face glowing with light from screen, big headphones turning him into Princess Leia.

Screech. The sound comes from me.

Son: why can't you leave me alone? I didn't seek this conflict. (Seriously.)

Flinch.

Go to bed, I say to him.

Go to bed, he says to me. You look tired.

You look tired. We say it to each other.

Okay, fine. He stands. Cracks his back luxuriously, in no hurry, as the computer winds down.

He's really smart. But what for? His braininess is as useless as my beauty was. I walked into a restaurant, knowing I was the prettiest woman there. He gets good grades.

I'm the best in my class, Mom. What do you want from me?

I want you not to play video games until 4am.
Do something else with your gifts.

Bitch.

Dark secret. He hits me. When he finally heads to bed, he whacks me above my ear. Tomorrow, the shower water blasting down will hurt my bruised scalp.

Ha ha, I say to myself, alone in the kitchen, hearing his bedroom door creak shut. He's boring. You're boring, son. Dad.

How much do you weigh?

116, Dad.

You look tired, bitch. Your face looks dragged down.

Yeah, I was pretty, but guess what? I read books that weren't required. Because I wanted to. He levels.

Simone Martel is the author of a book of creative nonfiction, The Expectant Gardener. Her shorter nonfiction has appeared in Greenprints and other magazines. Her stories have appeared in The Long Story, Short Story Review, Fogged Clarity and Magnolia Review.

Robert E. Petras

Robert E. Petras is a graduate of West Liberty University and a resident of Toronto, Ohio. His fiction and poetry have been published in numerous magazines, including The Camel Saloon, The Second Hump, Eunoia, Blue Collar Review, Howls and Pushycats and State of Imagination.

GRAY WINDOW

Staring through a window beaded with rain,

I see raindrops as big as eyes,

eyes like tumors—

blind, blank and bloated—

seeing only grayness,

grayness that becomes grayer

as in the depths of a river.

It is the color between nothing and black.

It is the color inside closed eyelids.

It is a sound of a never-ending tunnel.

It is a gray mass—cold, dark and growing.

A raindrop trickles down the window

and is swallowed in gray.

Frank S. LeRose

Other than what is contained in his decade long publishing history, Frank S. LeRose feels there is nothing else of himself to tell.

In Grey Days,

there is always
another time
to die through
solitude,
that which bends,
the outside world,
wherever-
I go; I'm still
there
frozen in motion.

Trichloroethane

Apt to know nothing
anymore than
a swear to atrophy
in deep breaths,
the oracle of the subconscious,
and the "why" birds have hollow bones.

Servants Of Disgrace

Ever suffer
the act to out
harbored shame
in ways, so misunderstood
they are named: disgrace
as always,
put upon within
without reason,
continuing to develop
the self-inflicted
children.

Featured 🗆🗆🗆 Poet
Michael Mc Aloran

Fall/Winter 2013

Michael Mc Aloran was Belfast born, (1976). His most recent work has appeared in ditch, Gobbet Magazine, Ink Sweat & Tears, Ygdrasil, Establishment, Carcinogenic, Primal Urge, A New Ulster, etc. A second full length collection, 'Attributes', was published by 'Desperanto' in 2011. 'Lapwing Publications, (Ireland), also published a collection of his poems, 'The Non Herein', in 2012 & The Knives, Forks & Spoons Press, (U.K), will release 'Emblems' and also an ekphrastic book of text/ art, 'Machinations' later this year. He also has two projects forthcoming from Quarter After Press...He edits Bone Orchard Poetry, a webzine of the bleak/ the dark/ the surreal and the experimental...

#9-

Echo within echo within shadow of...
Absence/ walls/ flames/ still breath alone

Pantheon of carousel/ of vertigo/ of absences

Night's undoing was never night
Hence the laughter forever ceases to be

#11-

Unto shadow/ dread...a poison key
Catacomb kiss...the ease by which/ lapsed

Shattered veins of sun/ night without traces
Foliage of skin/ expired meat/ drained of nothing

#14-

Danse of polka winds...night undone/
Night flourishing...

Silent retrace of bone/ vapours/ memories

Immense sky of non-death/ nothing lessened
Razor absences/ peeling away the bloodlessness

#15-

Hollowed tongue...winds dealt/ silenced
Dread lest the fingers break/ (only the elapsed)

Sing elixir of non-speech/ mouth full of dry sands
Leaving behind the drapery of skinned tide

#16-

Bleed...(where the stitched wind surrogates)
Night's laughter/ sonorous abandon...

Here and there...back then to follow/ breach
Again all over it and naught lest to follow/ done

#25-

Reek unto assuaged....
Skinned breath sharp as shock/ absent

Reek of dead silences/ earthen splendour

Back again till naught and the obscene scatter of...
Dead again...a burning forest of silences

Featured ▯▯▯ Poet/Photographer
Mark Burchard

Fall/Winter 2013

Mark Burchard, a former Motion Picture Costumer, was inspired by the slaphappy moments in his 29th film, "The Silence of the Lambs," to try his hand at writing comedy. He quickly moved on to include poetry, fiction, and memoir. His work has appeared in THE BATTERED SUITCASE, WESTWARD QUARTERLY, AUDIENCE MAGAZINE, LITTLE EPISODES, KEROUAC'S DOG, DO HOOKERS KISS?, SKIVE MAGAZINE, and THE STRAY BRANCH.

Mark's photographs were shown at the launch of Little Episodes in London, and can be seen on the covers of The Stray Branch and WestWard Quarterly. They also appear within the pages of Audience Magazine, The Battered Suitcase, and The Stray Branch.

Mark's filmography can be found at IMDB.com.

FREE

Was it your precious ego
Or were you too much of a man
That caused you to reject me
When you found out who I am?

Your mind was very narrow
For a guy who knew it all
For a man with all the answers
'Cept for one thing that's so small

There are no carbon copies
Of anyone I know
So what's wrong with being different
You angry so and so?

You were a married ladies' man
On that you had no peer
Is that what gave you the right
To name me your, "Little Queer?"

I never got inside your head
So I guess I'll never know
What caused the hate to buildup
In your lone and callused soul

Unchained today from all the shame
'Bout what you thought of me,
Cause on the day you met your maker
I'm the one who was set free

ON LEAVING

For twenty-four years I didn't see him
There was plenty of cause and lots of reason
Face-to-face he was on the attack
He beat me with a belt on my back

The first of his ten to take a stand
I grabbed that belt right out of his hand
"Kill me if you want," I shouted with dread
"I'd be better off cold and lying here dead!"

Screams in the night of impossible deeds!
"You're nothing more than a mouth to feed!"
Women and drinking were his kind of play
As the dreams of my childhood drifted away

I couldn't abide his swaggering ways
Or the guilt dealt out on holidays
That house never felt to me like a home
I had no choice but to leave and to roam

As a young man I was out on the run
Not many choices, what else could be done?
Trembling for hours in the cold drifting snow
I searched and prayed for a place to go

I moved to a city along side a lake
No more reasons to cry or to quake
But when that fair city proved much to close
I flew to the Apple on the far Eastern Coast

Heaven on earth, nothing could compare!
A whole new world opened for me there
Yet after those years without hearing from him
I'd weep at the thought of what could have been

But today I'm no longer in mourning,
Since I stepped from that stifling haze,
On the day I tossed the ghost of him
Into an all-consuming blaze

AFTER MIDNIGHT
An Illustrated Poem by Mark Burchard

After the bells sound midnight
When shadows no longer fall
Hallowed figures look down on us
From their lofty stalls.

Stoic figures
Of famous men,
With eroded faces
That cannot grin.

In cemeteries,
Cherubs
With out-stretched wings,
Stifle the dirges
They dare not sing.

Ancient scribes
Keep the toll
Of atrocities fashioned
From human souls.

Wrought from steel
Or carved from stone
From ancient Greece
Or noble Rome
Forged in the East
Or places unknown
Rest assured
You are never alone.

Forced by the Fates
To keep watch by night,
Enslaved by the madness
Of human delights;
Murder and thieving
Raped and bleeding
Stabbed and dying,
For their lives
They are pleading.

To close their eyes
And look away,
It's what effigies ask for
As they pray.

Sad,
But the gods hold at bay
The pleas of those wrought
From stone and clay.

So throughout the ages this stately band
Will, for as long as there's a grain of sand,
Watch humanity and rightly grieve
And silently lament on bended knee.

Michael Lee Johnson

Michael Lee Johnson is a poet and freelance writer and small business owner of custom imprinted promotional products and apparel: www.promoman.us, from Itasca, Illinois. He is heavily influenced by: Carl Sandburg, Robert Frost, William Carlos Williams, Irving Layton, Leonard Cohen, and Allen Ginsberg. His new poetry chapbook with pictures, titled From Which Place the Morning Rises, and his new photo version of The Lost American: from Exile to Freedom are available at: http://stores.lulu.com/promomanusa. The original version of The Lost American: from Exile to Freedom, can be found at: http://www.iuniverse.com/bookstore/book_detail. asp?isbn=0-595-46091-7. New Chapbook: Challenge of Night and Day, and Chicago Poems, by Michael Lee Johnson: http://www.lulu. com/product/paperback/challenge-of-night-and-day-and-chicago-poems-%28night%29/12443733. He also has 2 previous chapbooks available at: http://stores.lulu.com/poetryboy.

Michael has been published in over 23 countries. He is also editor/publisher of four poetry sites, all open for submission, which can be found at his Web site: http://poetryman.mysite.com. All of his books are now available on Amazon.com: http://www.amazon.com/s/ ref=nb_ss_b?url=search-alias%3Dstripbooks&field-keywords=michael+lee+johnson. Borders: http://www.borders.com.au/book/lost-american-from-exile-to-freedom/1566571/. Now on You-Tube: http://www.youtube.com/watch?v=Ih5WJrjqQ18. E-mail: promom-anusa@gmail.com. Audio Mp3 poems available; open to interviews. Follow Michael Lee Johnson On:

Facebook: http://www.facebook.com/poetrymanusa
Twitter: http://twitter.com/poetrymanusa
MySpace.com: http://www.myspace.com/469391029

Cold Gray

Below the clouds
forming in my eyes,
your soft eyes,
delicate as silk warm words,
used to support the love I held for you.

Cold, now gray, the sea tide
inside turns to poignant foam
upside down, separates-
only ghosts now live between us.

Yet, dream like, fortune-teller,
bearing no relation to reality-
my heart is beyond the sea now.
A relaxing breeze sweeps
across the flat surface of me.
I write this poem to you
neglectfully sacrificing our love.
I leave big impressions
with a terrible hush inside.
Gray bones now bleach with memories,
I'm a solitary figure standing
here, alone, along the shoreline.

-2007-

Even as Evening

Even as evening
approaches night-
dandelions shake
dust loose from their yellow-
a robin pulls
the last red worm
from the moist,
but callous
ground,
shadows fade
into fresh fall night-
small creatures
with trumpet
sounds dominant
the adjacent
woods.
A virtuoso!

-2010-

I Know from My Bed

Sometimes I feel
like a sad sack-
a worn out old man
with clown facial wrinkles.
I know when I reflect,
stare out my window
at the snow falling
from my bed,
my back to yours,
reflecting on my pain-
ignoring yours-
I isolate your love,
lose your touch
to another-
forgetting,
it is our bed,
not mine,
that I lie in.

-1999-

~   ~   ~

Tuesday Night Bowling
Fiction by Lily Murphy

Alex was sitting at home watching TV. It was Tuesday night which meant that there was not much
to do but sit at home and watch TV. Alex had his paunchy body slugged into the arm chair. There was
some sort of game show on TV but Alex wasn't interested. He gave his balls a scratch and then released
a fart. Suddenly his smoking addiction caused a sore sensation in his mind. 'I need a smoke' he muttered
to himself while rubbing the grubby stubble on his middle aged face.
Alex searched the pockets of his tattered old Levis and then his shirt pocket but found no familiar
packet of red Marlboros. He rubbed his stubble ridden chin again.
'Smokes' Alex howled out to Maureen who was busy in the Kitchen trying to stitch a hole in one of his
work shirts. She did hear him but ignored his cry for cigarettes. After so many years married to Alex she
developed a tough ignorance for him. 'I need some fucking smokes!' Alex howled out louder this time. 'I
got none, go fuck off' Maureen screeched back from the cramped kitchen as she continued sowing the
grubby work shirt which stank of car oil and manly sweat.
If Maureen were a flavour she would be sour and Alex would be tangy. He gave a heavy sigh and then
sprang up from his chair onto his feet. 'I'm going down to Mulligan's to get a packet of smokes' he
informed Maureen while reaching for his jacket hanging on a hook behind the front door. 'Don't you
dare fall in that door drunk out of your small fucking mind later on' she snarled out. 'Suck on it' Alex
growled back as he checked his pockets to see how much money he had.
'Why can't you wait until tomorrow to go get your fucking smokes?' Maureen stated while
scrunching her wizened little face. 'You know your mother must have fucked a hedgehog to produce
a prick like you!' she yelled to Alex from her place at the kitchen table. Alex opened the door. 'There is
nothing fucking worse in life than an argumentative wife' he shouted back but not before giving the
door a good bang on his way out.
Alex tramped the short walk down the road to his local watering hole. His black battered Doc Martins
pounded the gritty ground beneath him as coins jingled in the back pocket of his jeans.
As he made his way through the doors of Mulligan's, a guttery local bar, security was established in his
mind as he made a dart in the direction of the cigarette machine.
Alex's old friend and fellow bowling enthusiast Michael was hanging at the bar when he spotted Alex.
Michael coerced him to come to the bar and have a drink with him, just the one. 'I need a drink because
that hay bag of a woman wrecks my head' Alex said as he saddled up to the bar. 'Oh a bad wife is a
cancer to a good husband' Michael half heartedly laughed as he flung his arms around Alex. 'Have a
drink my old chum and you will soon forget your wifely woes.'

Thirteen beers later and Alex woke up with the pounding hammer of a hangover belting at the walls of his brains. Beer, and lots of it, tends to blow Alex's head apart thus causing a loss of memory.

He struggled out of bed and hit the floor face first. It was a wooden floor, his own bedroom floor was a carpeted one. Alex wondered where the hell he was and then restored himself to his feet. He cautiously turned around and saw that the woman in the bed he had just fell out of was not his wife and that the bedroom wasn't even his own.

Panic set in as he found his jeans scattered across the floor and he desperately tried putting them back on over his trembling legs. The woman in the bed began groaning and eventually opened her eyes which were smashed stale with mascara. Her peroxide blonde hair shone too brightly for Alex to look directly at so he kept his back to the strange woman.

Alex stammered and stuttered through a number of questions he gave to the strange woman, all the while keeping his back to her. Questions such as how he ended up in her bed and not his own and how he woke up next to her and not his wife. The woman flatly explained to Alex that he had gotten extra friendly with her after one too many Budweiser's and decided to end the night at her place. Enquiring of his friend Michael, Alex was told he was left snoring face down on the bar after talking himself into a drunken sleep.

'Your friend has a great philosophical tongue on him' the blonde haired woman suggested in a croaky tone of voice. 'You should have heard the stuff he was babbling on about' she laughed a course laugh. 'Yeah that's Michael for you, a man of rare intelligence, he rarely fucking shows it' Alex said while thinking of ways to throttle his old friend who coerced him into having just the one drink.

Through his bruising hangover which would go on to rack him for the rest of that day, Alex had a sudden burst of inspiration. 'Have you any talcum powder?' he asked the woman who was sitting up in bed and lighting a cigarette. She pointed lazily to a dresser at the other side of the room. Alex dashed over to it and put some talcum powder on his hands. Before the woman could ask him what he was doing, he had picked up his Doc Martin shoes and promptly left.

Alex went home to where his wife Maureen was waiting for him with a gruff expression stretched across her face. 'Where the fuck have you been all night? ALL FUCKING NIGHT!??' she demanded to know. 'I was in another woman's bed' Alex replied with all honesty. 'Don't you fucking lie to me!' Maureen screamed. 'I know you went out bowling with the boys again, I can see the powder on your hands!!!'

Lily Murphy is 25 and comes from Cork city, Ireland. Email: lilymurphycork@gmail.com

Paul David Adkins grew up in South Florida and lives in New York.

MRS. SAVOY MAKES THE BRUSHES

This is the handle.
Here are the bristles.
These are the fingers
which fit them together.

These are the palms,
which close on the pennies I earn.

Would you pronounce this wage of mine
a living?
Waking at five,
retiring at twelve.
Bristles litter the floor.
The handles I break
I must pay for.

My knuckles pop in the evening
like paper in burning trash.

Last night I scrubbed my calluses.
Dirt still shows.

This is the handle
that cannot be broken.

Here are the bristles.
None can be lost.

Featured Artist: Amanda Turco

Heart's War

Amanda Turco resides in Sault Ste Marie, Ontario, Canada. She is a portrait artist, reference library worker, and a mean coffee maker (although she doesn't drink the stuff). A drawing of hers came in second place in the Art Instructional School art competition, and was then published in their magazine, Illustrator, in 2007. In August of 2012 another painting of hers was featured in the literary magazine Black Lantern Publishing.

amandat396@hotmail.com

TSB/24 ~ ARTWORK / *Amanda Turco* ~ A Love Beyond

TSB/25 ~ ARTWORK / *Amanda Turco* ~ Burden of Responsibility

TSB/26 - ARTWORK / *Amanda Turco* - chickadee 2

TSB/27 - ARTWORK / *Amanda Turco* - Daemon

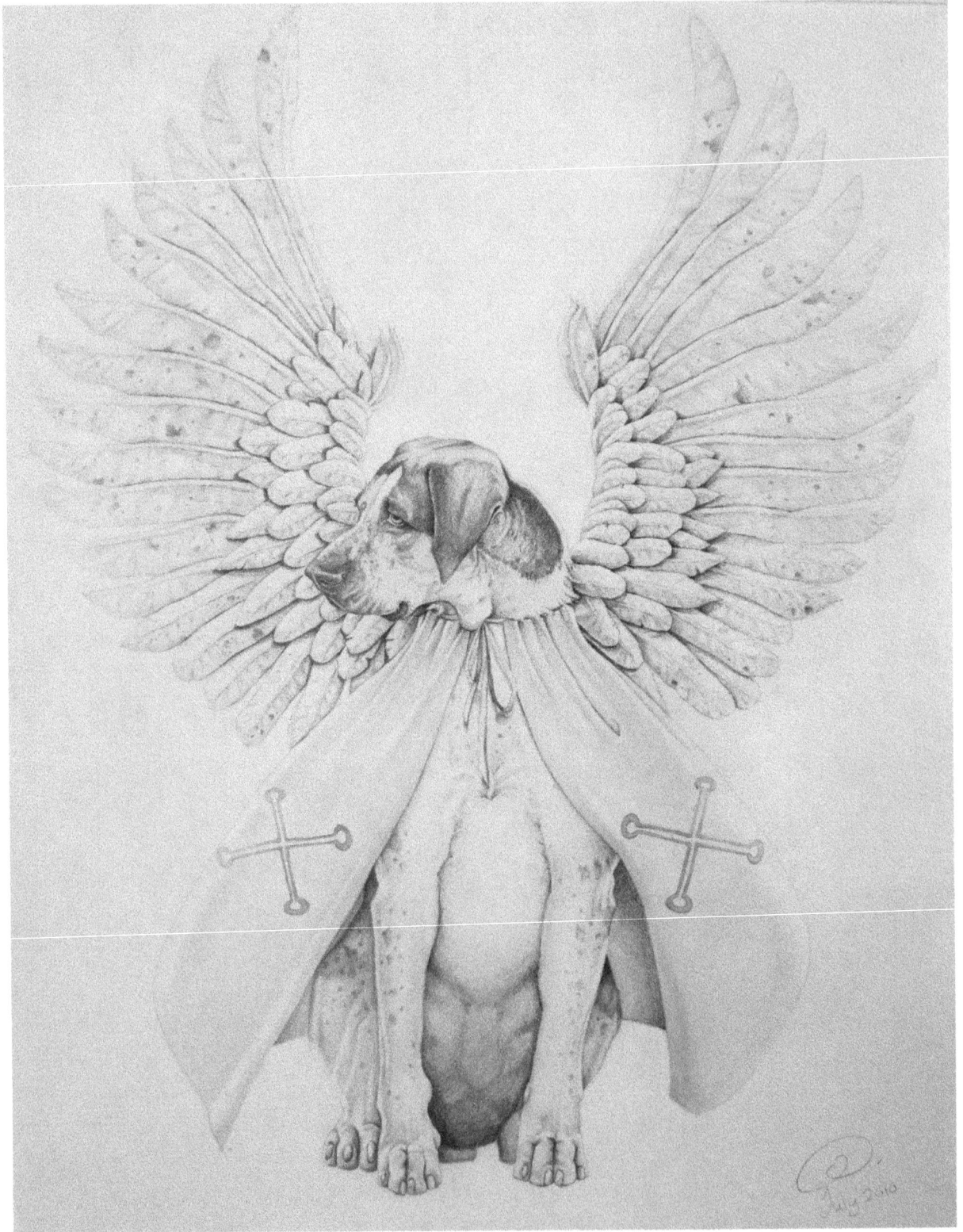

TSB/28 - ARTWORK / *Amanda Turco* - Jack

TSB/29 - ARTWORK / *Amanda Turco* - Loss of Innocents

Featured □□□ Poet
Annie Neugebauer

Fall/Winter 2013

Annie Neugebauer is a short story writer, novelist, and award-winning poet. She has work appearing or forthcoming in Wichita Falls Literature and Art Review, Six Sentences, Texas Poetry Calendar 2011, Voices de la Luna, Versifico, Eunoia Review, and Encore. Annie is the President of the North Branch Writers' Critique Group as well as the Vice President of the Denton Poets' Assembly. She lives in Denton, Texas with her husband Kyle and cat Buttons.

Get Over

I sit down at my desk
and rip the bandage off,
exposing the old wound
to open air.
As I type I feel something sticky,
viscous—
It's ointment, I tell myself—
but as the memory oozes
onto the screen
in shockingly neat lines of type,
I feel the sting,
as raw as if it were yesterday,
and I know there's no ointment...
only a redder type of ooze.

8/24/10

Deceptive Passages

When dad went to rehab, I tried
to hope, but still be well aware
that good statistics aren't applied
in every case, though it's not fair.

He didn't go just anywhere,
out of respect for his deep pride,
and though it's hard not to despair,
when dad went to rehab, I tried.

I wasn't sure how to divide
my thoughts between caution and care,
just like a magic trick inside:
to hope but still be well aware.

When he came home, broken and bare,
something deep inside me died;
the vodka on his breath declared
that good statistics aren't applied.

Not that this was the first time I'd
been given chances to prepare,
but no matter what, I still cried
in every case, though it's not fair.

The people at that clinic swear
that of the patients who complied,
relapse remains extremely rare,
although it sounds just like they lied—
when dad went to rehab.

1/27/10

Anxiety

I'm tired
of writing
in fragmentary lines,
words that don't rhyme,
subjects that don't matter,
thoughts that don't
weigh
anything.
So afraid to put my pen down,
to try,
to turn potential into proof
or failure.
I feel absolutely, physically sick,
my stomach writhing
like a bag of bugs,
at the thought
that I'm not good enough...
that I don't have the guts
to spill my guts,
red and bloody,
onto this thin, barren,
pathetically pristine
piece of notebook paper—
three holes in the side—
and that all I'll be left with
is a tired stream-of-consciousness poem
with a few bright spots
and far too many
short words.

~ ~ ~

THE SWARM
Fiction by Mark Slade

We were standing on the street corner where the docks were. Lots of Sailors came and went, looking for a good time. Kay spotted one sailor carrying his duffel bag on his shoulders walking past us. She pointed at him, told me to get his attention. I ran to him, using all of my sales pitch I've learned from the other pimps through the years.

Kay and I had been together for a long time, inseparable. She is a very pretty girl, when she wasn't on. That brings a lot bad facial expressions and dark circles creeping up. Her blonde hair down and in waves, angular face accommodating blue eyes, a favorite among johns. Especially in that short black dress.

I caught the sailor. Told him about Kay. He smiled big, said he wasn't sure about the price. I assured him for that price he would get everything he wanted. He didn't need a room, we already had one.

That may have helped with the hook. He followed us back to our place at the end of the street, behind the coffee shop and dealership. He didn't seem nervous inside the room. On the street he kept watching to see if anyone was following. In the room, he was all over Kay.

She took her clothes off, stood by the bed. He asked if I was going to stay and watch. He made a crack about how small I was, called me a dwarf. Kay told him I had to stay close, for protection. He took his clothes off, tried to ignore the situation.

The sailor went to Kay, touched her breasts, kissed each one. He reached up to kiss her when her eyes had went hollow. Her mouth left open as gaping hole. A swarm of yellow jackets exited her eyes and mouth, congregated upon the sailor's body, drilling thousands of tiny holes inside of him.

I covered my ears to mute his screams.

It wasn't long that the swarm had taken bits and pieces of the sailor and stored the nourishment inside their stingers. They headed back to the nest deep inside of Kay's body, via her eyes and mouth.

I removed my hands from my ears, watched the sailor's skeletal remains slump to the floor, every bit of his flesh missing.

Kay sat on the bed, sighed. With her fingernails, she spread apart the skin that covered her breasts and chest cavity. Showing me a dark chasm. I crawled toward the bed, climbed. She had her eyes closed, so I stole a kiss. I crawled inside of her and watched the darkness envelope me as she closed her skin around me. I waited for the yellow jackets to bring me my food.

Every Mother would do this for her son.

Mark Slade lives in Williamsburg, VA with his wife anddaughter. He has been published in Burial Day.

After a rather extended and varied second childhood in New Orleans (street musician, psych-tech, riverboat something-or-other, door-to-door poetry peddler, etc.), Matt Dennison finished his undergraduate degree at Mississippi State University where he won the National Sigma Tau Delta essay competition (as judged by X.J. Kennedy). He currently lives in a 105-year-old house with "lots of potential" and can be reached at columbusmatt@cableone.net.

Recent poetry acceptances:

Rattle, Spoon River Poetry Review, Cider Press Poetry Review, Night Train, Natural Bridge, A Cappella Zoo, G.W. Review, Main Street Rag

Il Connoisseur Sanguinante

"Actually," said Death, pausing to wipe
his bony chin, "I find that I miss the old
method of flavoring. What was it called?"
he asked, rattling fork on finger bones.
"Marvelous aroma, if memory serves,"
he added, glancing hopefully up the
length of table stretched to everlasting.
But on hearing no reply from his ravenous
companions, only the clack of knives
on china, he fell silent. "Unfiltered!"
he cried out, sitting up straight. "Un...*filtered*,"
he sighed, savoring the word's invocation
of better days. "It was strong, I tell you,
possessed of an imperishable integrity.
It presented a challenge, of sorts;
you felt larger when it was over, pierced
with the incessant rhythm of Earth's eternal
depth and darkness, unlike this... *soup*,"
he ended, gesturing at his plate. "Ah, well,"
he sighed as he cracked another ribcage
and speared the soft, brown morsels which
he inspected with a wary eye before
popping them into his mouth,
"life goes on."

(Previously published in The Spoon River Poetry Review, 2007)

Starting in Cincinnati, still entrenched in the Midwest, Michael M. Marks was schooled during the cold war/fallout shelter era evolving to anti-Vietnam war college days, from Elvis to the Rolling Stones. The first of the baby-boomers, he is the middle child of five born in a six year span, always fighting to be heard. Now seriously younger than each of his own five children, he approaches the fiftieth celebration of his fifteenth birthday.

Meteorror Horror

The moon is still full to somewhere in space.
Gone are the dime stores, soda fountains, and gas station garages;
The fool is still attune to someone in place
To sucker him with confrontation barrages
Of hatred worn like a baseball broken pane.
How much time is really mine after
Committing my life to mundane
Breathing sweating peeing sleeping laughter?
Gone are the dinosaur downtown picture shows
And the midtown fluorescent automats, while
Only the cracks in the sidewalk oppose
My dimmer switched-on spotlight smile.
Medicine, economy—all a mystery.
The glassed-in phone booths my certain history.

MMM

Featured ⬚⬚⬚ Poet
Philip Tinkler

Fall/Winter 2013

Philip Tinkler was born in the bucolic north of England. He has been published in the Mad Hatters' Review, Red Fez, Word Riot, The Dream People, and Six Sentences. He lives in NYC with his words and woman. More ramblings can be found at philiptinkler.com

PSEUDOCIDE IN CLUB 27

We carry suicide notes
for every occasion
a bopping night eternal
of jazz-eyed rage

Rose petal midnights
and hearts of onyx
a moment of meaning
and moaning in morrows

Amber Koneval

Amber Koneval is a twenty year old Colorado native and a junior in college at Regis University, double majoring in Honors-in-English and Religious Studies. She began writing seriously in her sophomore year of high school and has been published in school literary magazines (Apogee and Farsighted) for five years running. In 2011, Amber won the 'Best Poetry/Prose' in that year's edition of the Apogee out of Regis University for her poem 'Use Templates in Your Essay'. She has also been published in print editions of Time of Singing, The Storyteller, The Wayfarer and Crack the Spine, with pieces scheduled for the Radix, The Poet's Word, and devozine as well as online through MOLT, Exterminating Angel and Atticus Review. She is also excitedly anticipating the release of her first full collection of poetry, Drunk Dialing the Divine due out from eLectio publishing late 2012.

Blood Splatterpaint

my mouth was too small
for big words
my ears too swollen
to receive them

but my head was so full
of ideas
it threatened to pop
like a carnival balloon

So God gave me paintbrushes for hands
so I could dip them
in my brain
and splatter my ideas
on a canvas

to save my weary head
from explosion
and my family
from cleaning up the mess

Action spurs creativity

*A dark commentary
by Shane Armstrong*

Are you ever going to tell her?

"No man, she would never understand."

Yea but if you don't tell her she's just going to wonder.

"I've got that covered."

Got what covered? The sheets?

"No. My girl."

One of us needs to go burn those sheets.

"I'll do it just let me finish here."

Why do you do this?

"I have to."

But do they always need to be so young?

"The more life left the more energy released."

It's kind of sick.

"No it's not."

She's dead.

"It wouldn't work if she wasn't?"

Why do we have to stay? I mean once it's done, why sit here?

"You have to understand. It offers a different perspective."

It's different alright.

"If it bothers you then go burn the sheets."

You said you were going to do it.

"That was before you called me sick."

I didn't call you sick.

"You'll have to try it sometime."

Eh, I'll pass.

"As the life wanes the words flow."

I can't do it. I need time.

"You can be quick about it."

Naw dude, I can't.

"That's not what Cynthia said."

That's not fair.

"Life's not fair. Besides at least I am showing some respect; capturing it."

Respect? Capturing it? You took it. It's just weird.

"Weird? You're standing in a pool of blood and just now you think it's weird."

Yeah.

"Yeah?"

I'm not like you. And when did you talk to Cynthia?

"Earlier; covering this afternoon with my girl. You're a pansy you know that?"

After what I just helped you do you're going to call me a pansy.

"What did you do? You stood there with your mouth hanging open."

What the hell? I backed you up!

"If standing around is backing me up, I'm sure as hell not bringing you along anymore."

Come on man.

"I don't do this for you. I'm under a deadline. Action spurs creativity."

Fine you keep doing it. I'm going to go burn the sheets.

"Remember, bottom of the stairs turn left."

When asked what he does Shane replies with a single word;
create. His art as been given solo shows; his writing has been
published and performed: create he does. A drop out of law
school, seminary, and the ever ubiquitous MFA program,
Shane uses his mind to make the world a better place.

In this piece he seeks to leave the graphics of the scene to the
reader; knowing what the mind will create can be far worse
than the actual meaning of the words.

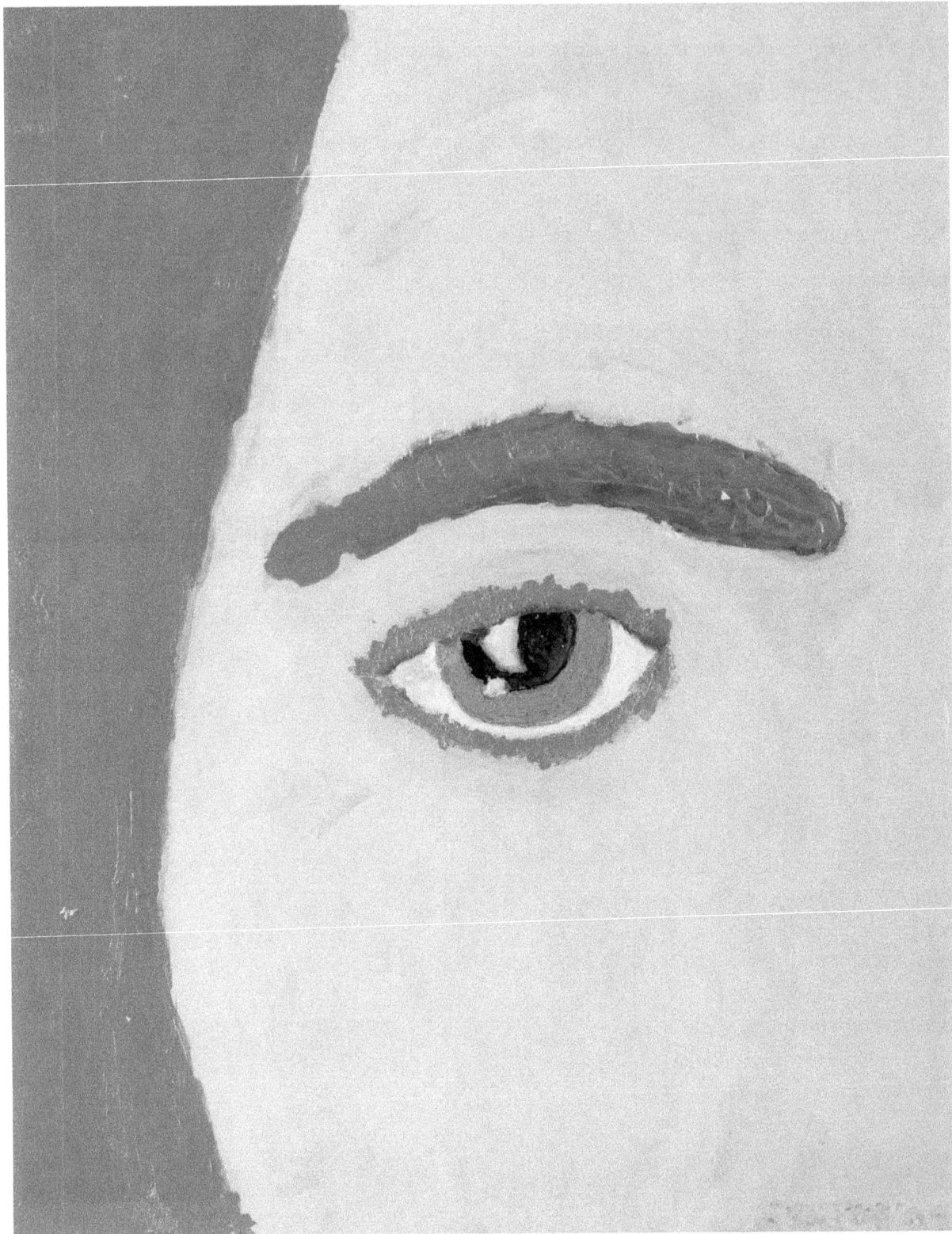

TSB/42 ~ ARTWORK / *Rex Sexton* ~ Eye Spy

Ivy's work has appeared in journals nationally, and anthologized. Her first book Any Other Branch, will be available through Salmon Poetry of Ireland in March 2012. Her second book, Elemental, will be out with Salmon Poetry in 2014. She is the editor and founder of Organs of Vision and Speech Magazine. For more about Ivy visit, www.poeticentanglement.com

Girl

At a young age
I learned the symbol:

circle head,
triangle body,
sticks for arms
and legs.

We aren't
beveled for the angles
provided.

But just
as I was taught
the symbol
for woman,
we are told,
molded to fit into some
semblance of
the symbol.

To Bring Me Home

You put linen sheets
the color of straw
around my body.

Behind me
a shadow,
black and white
easily simulated
charcoal drawing.

Girl—
I once thought
of as person.—
smudged,
fragmented,
a careless hand
sweeping across her.

At 14

Six feet tall, his hair
black silk, his
brown eyes that sparkled
like an imp.

He started talking
with an accent unlike
my own, and I was caught.
All my friends said
he was nice, and cute,
and I followed their lead.

He asked for my number
and I blushed
writing it in ink
on (I put a smiley face next to my name) a napkin.

He started talking.

       *

He had a blue
car and brown
eyes. He was four
years older, and drove
a motorcycle, played
bass guitar,
and was charming.

He spent hours
on the phone
with me, telling.

He asked my
parents if he could
take me out,
promised
to get me home
on time.

He never promised
I'd be safe.

Bird *(Featured Poem)*

He caught her.
She sang,
fragile figure captured.

Cold equivalent:
his violence,
her shape.

Hand

Fleshy palm
over closed eyes
your insulating voice,

drowned out.

I scream
feeling him
burning again.

Shaking, you take
your hand away.
All I see
is cold fire.

Sarah Anne Stinnett

Sarah Anne Stinnett was born into a family of artists. Poet, visual artist, thespian, and musician, she has plunged head-first into a multitude of disciplines of expression. As a senior at Berklee College of Music, Sarah has had her work published by FUSION Magazine. Simultaneously, she has been actively involved with the community of poets at Emerson College. In the spring of 2011 she received the honor of representing Berklee's student body by reading original works at the college's convocation ceremony.

The Broken Era

When feeling depressed I paint recklessly.

Iridescent havoc explodes upon

my canvas, a squinched orange or tomato

perhaps vermillion, I stab the fruit.

I break the fruit. Now perpetually

pungent I punish the fruit. It does not

struggle, my vexation overpowers.

At night in sleep the ocean beckons to

my tears, Come home. Come to rest my brothers.

I do not protest, freely they paddle

journeying back, down my cheek to the sea.

Then I paint big buildings with the lights on.

Big and bright and square and the lights are on.

Cut in half, as sandwiches, are they plunge

not yet smashed or squelched, static in midair

before the boom and the lights are all on.

Obliterating a world I create

I play God with fusions of rouge and blue.

Inextricable struggles consume my

acrylic nightmares. Tomorrow I'll paint

a ship, capsizing. The sea is it's tears.

Next, a girl with her eyes closed. Seemingly

untainted I've painted myself with no damage.

For now I've realized, I am the broken

Things I Didn't Know I Love

I didn't know how much I love

to hate tomatoes.

Dad grows his garden full every year

and year after year I basked in denying

consumption of those nasty motts.

Like digging out his weeds that sprout

it became habit for him to dig

at why I just wouldn't listen,

"eat your vegetables they're good for you."

Not just tomatoes. Broccoli, beans,

carrots, cauliflower, sprouts, asparagus, all planted

on my hate it list. Why is it

now that he's gone, I learned to love

what he always said was good for me?

My dad is a tomato plant,

Withered in winter, never to become unfrozen

he's in a palace of timelessness in the icing of snow.

I look for him every Spring,

waiting for buds to bloom with life.

I hate that he's gone. I tell myself

it's okay. Tomorrow

I'll be okay. Tomorrow will be

a better day. Tomorrow he won't delay.

Tomorrow will be great

Tomorrow I won't hate.

REVERIES

Happy & hung-over
I go to town in mid-afternoon in search
of aspirin I never find—instead, unusually quiet
streets. In Kizilay I find the street sellers
charming, the jewelry sellers, charming,
the tie-dyed shirt sellers, the fortune tellers.
I buy a packet of postcards
& a bootlegged tape. I marvel to myself,
how nice my new young friend
had been
to me.

       Scouring precincts that cling garden-like
& modern to the steeps of a lush ravine
below which mosques & basilicas line
the squares of a fine, busy town in ermine.
Sunk in a crushing doubleness, I read
& hope to recognize a scene no
longer there. I go along feeling
that I'm still breathing the same air,
until my heart aches & my lungs strain
against the emptiness.

OTOPATHY

you have become
a bare name on my lips—
name of a silenced emotion
remnant of an unanswered question
after the truth has been stretched
the elastic snaps back

your name
comes out of nowhere
speaking itself with nut-like persistence
unlooked-for recurrence
a gem of fire
suspended out of reach

like some strange reflex
calls and names all calls
through which I am called
as if heaven knows what
dialed me up
looking for you

part of me answering
out of part of you
as if yours was the name
in some half-forgotten language
for words I've now forgotten

Matthew Rodgers is a young poet, 24 years old. He is attending the New School University's program for Creative Writing. MFA. He has been writing for 2 years now. Matthew currently lives in New York City and San Francisco.

He has been published in the following magazines:

SFSU: Golden Gate Press February 2012
Tule Review, Sacramento, March, 2012
Ascent Aspirations, May 2011

Even At the End *(Featured Poem)*

The old woman sweeps the golden leaves
that have fallen on the streets into the gutter.
Somehow I feel as if she understands them.
Putting them to rest when there will be no one
to do the same for her. I remember once the
boy with a lions smile, who used to laugh at
the sighing trees. I have lost touch with him,
maybe he has turned to gold too. Last I heard
he was with his mother, but that was many
seasons ago, when even I could recall the
shadows of the Sun. But now, for what?
Sweeping the leaves into the street, when
there is nothing left to do, but make sure
that the ones who have fallen are taken care
of. Hopefully in peace, even though they may
not be seen again, you will know that you
loved them well enough, to see them off,
swaying in the breeze.

Elizabeth Swados

Elizabeth Swados is an award winning author and composer; she is a Tony nominated, Obie award winning theater artist, Guggenheim and Ford Foundation recipient, as well as a Pen/Faulkner citation. Her latest book, At Play – Teaching Teenagers Theater was published by Faber and Faber. Her other recent publications include: My Depression (Hyperion), and The Animal Rescue Store (Scholastic). Her theatrical credits span from Broadway, to off-Broadway, to around the world includingRunaways, Missionaries, and Jabu. Her poetry has appeared in magazines such as Meridian Anthology, New American Writing, New York Quarterly, Emory's Journal, Confrontation, Paterson Literary Review, Speakeasy, Barrow Street, Runes and Home Planet. Her first book of poetry, The One and Only Human Galaxy, was released in April 2009 and a book of non-fiction prose, Waiting, was released in late 2011.

No Control *(Featured Poem)*

In a dream
my body is floating along.
The current of
muddy water
pushes me downstream
as roofs and cars go by
on liquid trains
I can't catch up
to stop myself
and even if I could grab on
even by the sleeve of my shirt
I would only drag myself under,
Half drowning
trying to catch one shred of cloth
I fall deeper
into the vast and open brown
colored
thick and disappearing town.

Brendan Sullivan is a lifelong beach bum who has turned from acting to poetry, as he finds it a more remarkable muse. He also enjoys surfing, sailing and diving. His work has been published at Wordsmiths, The Missing Slate, Every Writer's Resource, Gutter Eloquence, A Sharp Piece of Awesome, After Tournier, Bareback Magazine and Bare Hands.

Torn

He felt the magic in his hands
and tasted the echo of colors
as his fingers ached across the keys
loving them like children
and notes filled the space
falling to the floor
echoing on the wood
the resonance of too many years
haunting the room
the tune trembling on his fingers
broke his heart
and swelled the ears
of all those who heard
the music of the torn.

Serial Boy

You never were very bright
mama said
as she boxed his ears
and served him another helping of corn pudding.
The boy never said a word
just continued to smash peas
with a dirty fork,
watching the tines pierce their green skin,
and burying them
under a river of gravy
that ran down the greasy plate.
But his eyes never left mama's face
as his fork tapped the chipped formica
and he felt her sickly sweet smile
roll down his cheeks
into the gravy
caught under his lip.

Confessional *(Featured Poem)*

My thoughts of her
hush the candles,
make the confessional go dark
and the priest's breath ragged.
I can hear it
slide down his throat,
and under his habit
I can hear
his skin disapprove
and prickle the long black robe
in ways that make me blush.
He demands
details on my tongue
of how she felt
and the color of her hair
as if that intercourse of words
crushed up into the dark

will break me like salvation.

Wires

I caught you
walking out on wires again,
falling out my window
in a trick so beautiful
that your father wept
and your lover
held his breath.
You called it
an act of defiance
in that voice
that brings me to my knees
and begs me
to argue with you
when you know
that all I really want to do
is strip the pain
from your insides
and bed you
like war.

Photography by Sally Burnette

Sally Burnette is currently a student at Eckerd College in St. Petersburg, Florida. She has been published in Poetica Magazine, Deep South Magazine, and the Eckerd Review

dragonfly

the dragonfly of despair,
fool,

knows of your sagging couch
and is pissing in the font
of your karmic dues

it's returning soon

the multi-winged
annihilator of a
thousand and one
different outcomes.

Verdict

You come to us through deed and little lies,
those without a trace of sustenance nor of
redemption: weeping, your incontinence,
some droll, a sob, mental tentacles of an
unending embrace and murmurings
of your true name.

~ ~ ~
# Body Bag
Fiction by Eric Bonholtzer

His wife was in the bag, well, what was left of her. Vincent had been able to get rid of one of the hands when he'd stopped for gas, providing a very hungry and very scrawny dog with a decent meal, and he knew that if he could just make it to Forester City, he'd be in the clear. His brother, Trevor, an undertaker, would burn up the leftovers in the crematorium oven, and then he'd be home free. Being the close brother that he was, Trevor was more than willing to help, especially knowing what that wretched wife had done to little Timmy.

Just as Vincent's blood was beginning to boil, the thought of what his wife had done making his skin blister, he heard the squeal of tires approaching from behind. His own car had broken down a few miles back, and a brief look under the hood confirmed the fact that the engine had finally died once and for all, the wife having always insisted any money saved for a transmission overhaul be spent on herself instead. With at least another thirty miles to go until he reached Forester City, Vincent stuck out his thumb, hoping to herald a ride, knowing that the sooner he disposed of his wife's body, the better. It was only too late that he realized, his thumb sticking out like a homing beacon, the runnel of dust set tling and the tires screeching to a halt, that he'd flagged down a county sheriff.

Just my luck, he thought bitterly, cursing everything that had brought him to this point. The car that had broken down, the person who he'd decided to spend his life with who'd destroyed everything he'd ever loved. Standing there, Vincent just wished he could go back in time, before the nightmare that had become his life. Back to when Timmy was still alive, when they were struggling, but surviving, in Jamestown, a place he could never return to again. It seemed to Vincent that life wasn't without a terrible sense of irony, because the cop's car that pulled up next to him bore the blazing insignia of the Jamestown County Sheriffs. Figures, Vincent thought. He'd only made it three cities away from home before the car died, unfortunately still within county lines. But the whole situation still made him seethe. It just wasn't fair.

"How y'all doin'?" the cop asked as he exited the car. "Awful hot out to be walkin', ain't it?" He was a burly man with a broad-brimmed cowboy hat that didn't seem to be doing its job, judging from the large lobster-red sunburn beneath both eyes. Now that the cop mentioned it, Vincent realized just how hot it really was. He was sweating profusely, and he prayed the sheriff didn't take that for a sign of guilt.

"Uh, I'm fine, actually. Just doin' a bit of travelin'." Vincent spoke with that same southern drawl the sheriff did. Having grown up and spent his entire life in Dixieland, it was as much a part of him as a love of grits and jazz, but the officer's inflection was far more pronounced, a good old boy if Vincent had ever seen one.

"Well, now, that's a relief. See, I thought you was in some trouble. Need a lift?" It was one simple question that put Vincent in one hell of a situation. If he accepted the ride, it was almost certain the cop would find out he had a body in the bag. But if he refused, especially after flagging the officer down, then it was almost certain that he'd be detained and searched, and that was completely out of the question.

It was a lose-lose situation, but Vincent figured that given the choice, he might as well spend his time in the cool air-conditioned confines of a police car, rather than sprawled spread eagle along the side of a dusty road. He gauged his chances of making a run for it and realized the futility. There was nowhere to go. Trying to keep the fear from his voice, Vincent smiled, "Appreciate it."

"Good. Could use a little company. Been investigatin' all mornin' and I jus' want a li'l human company to brighten my day. I saw a car a couple miles back, a clunker stashed off to the side of the road. That wouldn't be yers, now would it?"

Not knowing exactly what the cop knew, but hoping his plates hadn't been run, as he was probably the prime suspect in the disappearance of his wife, Vincent effected an air of nonchalance. "Nope. No car. Just out fer a li'l walkin' trip." The officer stared at him through reflective lenses, but said nothing. Vincent tried not to let the cop have any more time for questions as he scurried around the backside of the patrol car, hoping to drop the body as soon as possible. "Could ya pop the trunk?" Vincent swallowed hard when he heard the officer's response, "Oh, here, I'll take that bag fer ya." Vincent's stomach knotted, each footfall of the officer's seeming impossibly slow, realizing that it was the beginning of the end. And as the officer unlocked the trunk, Vincent was sure that the cop could smell the decomposition of his wife's body, could just feel that horrid offal stench pervading his nostrils, offending every olfactory sense. But the officer said nothing and merely took the bag and tossed it in the trunk.

Vincent swallowed hard when he heard the officer's response, "Oh, here, I'll take that bag fer ya."

Vincent's stomach knotted, each footfall of the officer's seeming impossibly slow, realizing that it was the beginning of the end. And as the officer unlocked the trunk, Vincent was sure that the cop could smell the decomposition of his wife's body, could just feel that horrid offal stench pervading his nostrils, offending every olfactory sense. But the officer said nothing and merely took the bag and tossed it in the trunk. Vincent could barely believe it, expecting at any second to feel the sting of handcuffs on his wrists, but the officer gave the bag no more than a second thought, slamming the trunk shut and getting into the car. Vincent, not wanting to press his luck or raise any more suspicion, hurried into the

the passenger seat as the cop fired up the engine.

After the initial question of Vincent's destination was answered, the two men drove for a few minutes in silence, the whole time the passenger convinced he could smell a permeable aura of death emanating form the trunk.

"Name's Zeek," the cop said, extending a meaty palm. Vincent took it quickly and shook it, praying that the cop wasn't sensing that same pungent odor he was now certain was filling the cabin of the car. "What's yours?"

"Mi..Micheal," he stammered.

"Mike, my boy, you don't know how good it is to be talkin' to another livin', breathin' soul. I've been investigatin' since early this mornin' an' I keep thinkin' I'm gonna go insane if'n I don't get some real human contact."

"So whatcha been investigatin'?" Vincent tried for anything that might divert the cop's attention away from questions about why his passenger had been walking along a deserted road carrying a suspicious looking package. Questions with no good answers. A sign in the distance provided a slight sliver of hope, "Forester City - 15 miles." Vincent knew if he could just keep Zeek's mind occupied for a few more minutes, he might be all right.

"Well, I was investigatin' a domestic call, back in Jamestown. Funny thing was, when I got there, wasn't no one home. But there was blood. Lots of it. Nowadays it's awful hard to prove some one's dead 'less we got a body, so that's what I'm on the troll fer. Car was gone too, and records say the missin' guy's got family in Forester City, so that's where I'm headed. And seems as if it's yer lucky day, now don't it, pardner?" Vincent couldn't help but cringe, his stomach churning, his hands growing clammier by the second. The cop was talking about him, there was no doubt about it. Zeek leaned in close, pulling off the reflective lenses as he did. "Y'all married?"

Vincent knew the end of the road when he saw it. This whole time, the cop had been toying with him. *Forester City. A clunker stashed off to the side of the road, that wouldn't be yers now would it?* The cop's words echoed in his head. *He'd known all along.*

Vincent still felt trapped, suffocated, the rancid smell from the bag in the trunk filling the air with pungent aroma too strong to be ignored. Knowing that he was a goner anyway, Vincent still decided not to give an inch, but instead to play along until the final card was dealt. "I'm recently widowed." He grinned sardonically to himself.

Strangely, Zeek was all sympathy. "Sorry to hear that."

Vincent could have either laughed or cried, sometimes that border becoming blurred. "Well, that makes one of us." As the cop shot him a strange look, he continued. "She was the most horrible person I've ever known. I hope she rots in a river of darkness. Gave me misery ever since I slipped that ring on her finger. Ya know, I worked two jobs jus' to feed our family and it wasn't never enough. She always took it out on our son, real abusive. I don't have no education. Could only do what I could. Would've done anything for that woman, but it weren't ever good enough. Ever."

"What happened?"

"Well, you could say she just went to pieces." Vincent couldn't help but chuckle, wondering if this was what it was like to stand on the brink of madness.

"Huh. Ya know, you look real familiar, pardner," Zeek said with his own smile.

Those words. The curtain was about to be drawn, the game most certainly up, like a Twilight Zone version of Let's Make a Deal where the only prize left was Death Row. Vincent was about to open his mouth to admit his guilt, tired of the whole charade, when Zeek spoke again.

"Now, I know it. That's who y'all look like. My partner investigated a case 'bout a month back, I seen the pictures. It was a mother who drowned her own son, 'cause they couldn't afford fer all three of 'em. Pure evil, she was. But man, if'n y'all don't just look like that husband. Said he was workin' at the time but he was sure she'd drowned the boy. But with no witnesses, we had to rule it an accident, even though he had so many bruises. Poor li'l boy. Timmy was his name. I'll never forget it." Zeek smiled, but there was no humor in it. "That's mighty funny, seein' as how y'all look so much like that man, 'n it was that woman's disappearance I was investigatin'."

Just get it over with, Vincent thought bitterly, the whole time feeling like he could just drift away, float off to somewhere peaceful where values were still held and things still made sense. The unreality seemed to sweep him up in its grasp.

Zeek continued on, as if nothin' was wrong. "But ya know what? If'n that husband ya look like had decided to get rid of that monster, I wouldn't be blamin' him one bit. I had a sister murdered 'bout fifteen years ago. Beautiful girl, killed by a drifter. She's the reason I became a cop. Never did catch the guy, he's still out there somewheres, but I'm watchin' fer him, always. My sister's with Jesus now, I know that sure as I know the sky's blue, but I tell y'all, much as I hate to admit it, even after all these years I'd give anything just to see the look in that bastard's eyes as I squeezed the life outta him. I know what that man felt like losing his son and I feel mighty sorry for him, but I wouldn't wanna be in his shoes. We got an eye out for him. We gotta nab him 'n bring him in, much as most of us don't want to. The law, ya know?"

Vincent hated the way Zeek was beating around the bush. *Yeah, great, y'all feel sorry for me. I'll think about that as I gather dust in a cell awaitin' my execution. Just do it already,* he nearly screamed within his own mind, *just slap on the cuffs and take me in. No more tauntin', no more tormentin'.* The smell of rotting flesh assailed his senses once again, seeming as if the cabin of the car had become filled with the oppressive stench of decomposition. The silence hung between them like a shroud.

"Well, here we are. I gotta go talk to the husband's brother," Zeek said with a grin, as he pulled to the side of the road. Vincent could see the funeral home in the distance outside his window, just past the meandering Muddy River that ran deep throughout the county. *So this is where it'll happen. This is where he's gonna get me, just a few feet from freedom.* He could almost taste the irony, bitter on the back of his tongue. But as Zeek opened the door and popped the trunk, Vincent didn't feel the sting of handcuffs being clenched down upon his wrists.

And as the cop handed over that bag, Vincent was sure that this was the coup de gras, to be the caught with bag in hand. Zeek merely smiled sadly and said, "Thanks fer the company." And even as drop of blood fell from the bag, landing between them, Zeek didn't seem to notice, leaving Vincent in the road, no cuffs, no questions asked.

As he walked away, waving all the while, Vincent could hear Zeek's parting words, ones which he took to heart. "Ya know, I think drowin' the bones in the Muddy River would be fittin'. And seein' as we already dredged it this mornin', I don't think nobody'll be lookin' there again. Just some advice, now. Take care, *Vincent*."

And as Vincent stood there on the side of the road under the sun's bright rays, the promise of a new day and a new start at hand, he gave a little prayer of thanks for everything that had happened and thanks that he had been fortunate enough to be left holding the bag.

Eric Bonholtzer is an attorney with a Master's Degree in English and a strong publishing history. Eric has established quite an audience with his short story work, and a collection of his short fiction entitled, The Skeletons Closet, was released to great acclaim. He won first place in both the fiction and poetry categories of the College Language Association (CLA) Creative Writing Contest/Margaret Walker Prizes for Creative Writing national competition. Eric is also the recipient of the Ted Pugh Poetry Award and took 2nd place in New York Times Bestselling Author F. Paul Wilson's "Stump Repairman Jack" Creative Writing Contest, among other honors. Several of his stories and poems have been included in anthologies. In addition to writing fiction, He writes for several prominent publications such as FIGHT! Magazine and Skinnie Entertainment Magazine, and he was a two-time finalist in the Rolling Stone "I'm from Rolling Stone" National Journalism Contest. Eric is a member of the Sigma Tau Delta English Honors Society as well as a member of the Moot Court Honors Program, Law Review, and the Trial Advocacy Honors Program.

~ ~ ~

Hands
Fiction by Terence Kuch

A subway car.

A young man is drawing in his sketch pad, making vigorous strokes with an art pencil. He is drawing a pair of hands.

Every few seconds he glances up to assure himself that the previous stroke was made in the right place, at the right length, with the proper intensity, to portray the hands of the old man who is sitting several feet away, facing him.

The pencil lead almost breaks. The young man detects the imminent catastrophe and eases his stroke just in time.

Hands are difficult to draw. The young man has not yet mastered the drawing of hands.

Faces are not so difficult for him, but he never looks at the old man's face.

The old man is observing the top of the artist's pencil, trying to divine the shapes being formed on the page he cannot see. He can tell from the young man's glances that his hands are being drawn.

The old man puts on a slight smile, ready to make eye contact.

The young man does not make eye contact.

The old man does not know whether to be flattered or bothered by his being an involuntary artist's model. He believes there is more to him than hands.

The old man thinks that the artist may have drawn not only his hands, but something else as well. This is his conclusion from observing the motions made by the top of the artist's pencil as it moves left, right, up, down, slow or fast, awry or straight.

The young man never looks anywhere but at the old man's hands and at his sketch pad.

There is a great silence between the two men, obscuring the noise made by the subway train.

FINALLY THE OLD MAN SAYS, may I take a look at your drawing? He says this in as friendly a tone as he can. He does not like to be thought of as one who objects. He wonders if the young man will show him the drawing, or refuse to, or run away, or slam his sketch book closed and say mind your own fucking business, or give the drawing to him, or ask for money.

THE YOUNG MAN SAYS, see. He turns the sketch book around. There are the old man's hands. They look older than the old man thinks they should. The hands look as if they might begin to shake any time now and never stop. In the drawing, the old man's right hand is holding a knife.

See, the young man says, it is a Vilshofener fixed-blade clip knife, with a prominent quillion and two-tone mirror polish satin finish. Its haft bears the mark of a famous maker of knives, long since dead. His workshop was in the Kleine Messergasse in Passau, just a short distance from the river and its boats. All the boatmen used his knives. For one purpose or another.

Why did you draw my hand holding such a knife, the old man asks.

I saw it there, says the young man. I saw your hand holding such a knife. That is why I drew your hands, to see what kind of knife you would be holding, and now I know. Now I know you.

Will you sell it to me?

My drawing?

No, the knife.

Terence Kuch is a consultant, avid hiker, and world traveler. His checkered publication/acceptance career includes Clockwise Cat, Commonweal, Dissent, Journal of Irreproducible Results, Marginalia, New York magazine, North American Review, Northwest Review, The Realist, Slow Trains, Thema, Timber Creek Review, Washington Post Book World, and Washington Post Magazine. He has studied at the Writers Center, Bethesda, Maryland, and participated in the Mid-American Review Summer Fiction Workshop.

Featured □□□ Poet
Bruce Millar

Fall/Winter 2013

An artist living and working out of Toronto, Canada, Bruce Millar writes in a rainbow of tones including everything from kid's poetry to erotica, humorous stories, musical parodies, meditation music, flash fiction and short stories.

Those Drinking Days

Beer mug
full of rye,
just enough ice
and ginger
to keep the bile down;

time on vcr
doubles, splits,
stretches farther apart until
tv becomes incomprehensible;

headphones
bandaged onto ears,
too wired to sort the wires;

urine stained mason jars
wait beside chair, as
makeshift chamber buckets;
too much piss
too much fear

too much flushing
will wake her up
and I'll be on the street;

pull arms along carpet,
bottle in one hand,
fist in the other;
drag body, rest;
drag body, rest
legs a liability;

onto chair in bedroom,
short fall to bed
past the bruises
and broken glass;

night turns into day,
day turns into nothing,
nothing turns into sunlight
and pesters closed curtains
like kids at an ice-cream truck;

dehydration necessitates levitation,
bathroom tap bleeds cold water,
not cold enough
to reach Loch bottom;

back to mattress
on floor,
fan on full blast
cuts down on white noise,
inside and out;

broke, sick, despondent,
eye puffed up and purple
from collision with table
and my own fist,

doesn't hurt as much as
the shame in my gut;

on a good day,
face the terror of the mailroom,
and hope they don't see
my eyes;

they'll know
how bad I am,

safer to go
in dead of night.

The darkness drinks as I do.

Timothy B. Dodd

Timothy B. Dodd is from Mink Shoals, WV. He fares well in caves, cenotes, and "forgotten" places. His writing has appeared or is forthcoming in Yemassee, Main Street Rag, The William and Mary Review, Metal Scratches, and A Clean, Well-Lighted Place.

<u>They Sent Him for Pills</u> *(Featured Poem)*

He will fall away,
eventually,
dissolve from hollowed insides,
the purpose hidden under a trapped lung,
some meaning lost in an overworked kidney,
both stashed in a deceased stranger's attic
beneath moldy clothes and hoarded trinkets,
covered more by neglect than by the elements

A profusion of phone chatter, profit margins, advertisements, cereal choices, bus routes,
platitudes, trivialities, billboard smiles
colonize imagination
shroud, numb, disfigure

"I looked for hope in a restaurant." (under your diamond ring)

Left to feed on desiccated leaves,
dropped tusks,
plastic dung

He will fall away
eventually,
and his body will store
only the bones and bags
that sleepwalk at noon,
await disease,
pay to release seed,
walk to extinction

He will fall away,
eventually,
like me

David Lawrence

Green House

You don't want to freeze the hose in the summer
Because meltdown is in the grass.
I ride a butterfly over your delicate pajamas
And go to sleep with you in the green house.
We plant ourselves in vases
And make of ourselves bouquets to the glass refracted sun.
We sell ourselves to tourist life
And become part of the recreation of stragglers.
We are an arboretum of colorful pansy emotions.
Let the sun play on the scratches of our roof glass.

SPOONING

I take out my eye and put it in a spoon.
It is a soft-boiled egg.
I eat my vision and it becomes insight.
I see the landscape inside myself and know
That I am part of the trees and the shrubs.
I am a psychological arboretum.
I bought a ticket.
I am a tourist.
I take fertilizer from my pockets and feed
The plants.
I am God.
I am responsible for someone else's garden.

ENDLESS PASSAGE

The bullet goes through you and out the other side.
You are a shot up thing.
Little darling,
It's hard to watch you bleed on the veranda
Beneath the waiters delivering their cocktails.
You are holy like the Catholic Church
Or Swiss Cheese.
You are lactose intolerant.
You feel the wounds like life's accidents.
You try to fill the holes with denial but just end up
Bleeding into death's affirmation.
Life is an artificial interruption in our endless passage.

Valentina Cano

Valentina Cano is a student of classical singing who spends whatever free time either writing or reading. Her works have appeared in Exercise Bowler, Blinking Cursor, Theory Train, Cartier Street Press, Berg Gasse 19, Precious Metals, A Handful of Dust, The Scarlet Sound, The Adroit Journal, Perceptions Literary Magazine, Welcome to Wherever, The Corner Club Press, Death Rattle, Danse Macabre, Subliminal Interiors, Generations Literary Journal, Super Poetry Highway, Stream Press, Stone Telling, Popshot, Golden Sparrow Literary Review, Rem Magazine, Structo, The 22 Magazine, The Black Fox Literary Magazine, Niteblade, Tuck Magazine, Ontologica, Congruent Spaces Magazine, Pipe Dream, Decades Review, Anatomy, Lowestof Chronicle, Muddy River Poetry Review, Lady Ink Magazine, Spark Anthology, Vine Leaves Literary Magazine, Avalon Literary Review, White Masquerade Anthology and Perhaps I'm Wrong About the World. You can find her here:http://carabosseslibrary.blogspot.com

A Drowning

This could not be heavier

if you forced it.

Three seconds,

bogged down by soggy thoughts,

are like stones in my pocket,

forcing me down,

so that the only things visible,

the only things I'll ever be

remembered for,

are the bubbles of air

dying in the sun.

Morning's Choice *(Featured Poem)*

She warns her to look away.

To peel eyelashes off the surfaces

they've caressed and marked

(fossils on a pillow).

She tells her to shift skin like a quilt,

right off the bed in a tumble.

Bu she won't listen,

or at least not now

when it means losing another limb

or perhaps another sliver of voice.

Time binds her and leads her on,

pulsing brilliant like a sun,

yet warming nothing.

First Day of Summer

That morning,

when the sky darkened

with ink leaking from my pen,

I didn't know what I'd do.

Days elongated until I was looking

at a hallway of sealed doors,

each as chilly as the next.

The sun,

wrapped in the violent sky,

disappeared.

I tried to make a hole in the darkness,

in the silence,

but all I got was a fistful of static.

EGYPTIAN NIGHT *(Featured Poem)*

I've shadowed my youth with

arms raised, dancing the full aroma of summer while my

feet discover unknown paths.

My skin feeds on the colors of day as I melt with warm

sand near waters of Egyptian green and blue; I strike

the surface with stones.

I have the day attached to me like magnets.

I carry the cloak of searching, turning corners wide eyed.

Night breathes in approaching shadows, beckoning gray

curtains of air opening the envelope of dusk, the first act of night,

shading the darkness until black is achieved.

"HEARTACHE IS A LONER"

I seek the woman for the love
that I never quite received
I sought the woman for the love
in any way to please
I found the woman for the love
for my love's a reprieve
I have the woman that I love
and loathe for I deceive

John David Muth

John David Muth is an academic advisor at Rutgers University. He writes when the mood sways him. He tries to publish every now and again. Sometimes, he is successful. Sometimes, he is not. If he can write a poem that readers can enjoy, he has done a decent thing.

Out With The Girls *(Featured Poem)*

She smells like vodka
And cigar smoke.

Through the fumes of
Public bathroom liquid soap,
Generic aftershave
And worn out latex
Try to confess.

Her T-shirt is wrinkled.
It looks like she broke
A couple of fingernails.
They are probably still in his back.

She tells me she was out with the girls,
Looks aggressive,
As if waiting for my contradiction.
I only reassure her
And suggest she take a hot bath.

My buttercup walks away self-assured.

In a few more minutes,
Water greased with middle-aged funk,
Spray-tanned skin,
And the hard plastic of a small TV
Will join in an orgy of electricity.

I'm gonna miss that TV.

Supper Alone

A whirlpool of blood
Rages in my stomach,
And the sound within my ears is desolation,
Like a medieval village
Crackling to death in the distance.

Sometimes,
I am wallpaper
Attached to a pitted surface
By glue that never dries.
The lightest touch
Will tear the pretty flowers.

Sometimes,
I am a long-forgotten howitzer shell
On a World War II beach
That her memory
Kicks into explosion.

I re-form,
Rusted and powder-charged,
At the very next moment.

The coffee and the soup are cold,
And I have no strength
To heat them in the microwave.

If I ever remember today,
When I'm in the arms of the next one,
It may cause a flush of shame.
If she asks, I'll tell her
I'm just happy she's mine.

It wouldn't be a total lie.
I hope.

Martin Willitts Jr.

Martin Willitts Jr was recently nominated for two Best of The Net awards and his 5th Pushcart award. He has four new chapbooks: "The Girl Who Sang Forth Horses" (Pudding House Publications, 2010), "Van Gogh's Sunflowers for Cezanne" (Finishing Line Press, 2010), "True Simplicity" (Poets Wear Prada Press, 2011), and "My Heart Is Seven Wild Swans Lifting" (Slow Trains, 2011).

Why Can't I Remember

Why can't I remember,
negative emotions are always workable?
Why does an ant mound before a rain remind me
to work on impossible things in the face of impossible odds?
I was shucking corn and yanking so hard
it might have cried if I had been listening.
But the sorrow I felt was so overwhelming, all I could do
was yank until the husks turned blue.
There is absurdity in wanting more,
but I was in the sadness trying to pull myself out.
The orchids would be still white outside, no matter what I did.
They would eventually wilt and disappear
and I might miss it; but I was too busy wrenching.
What was at stake here?
I hardly noticed what I was doing. I was so lost.
It is possible to lose something and still have something.
We need the leisurely time to do nothing to find it.
What I think is mine, and mine alone,
is something anyone can have.
When I stripped the cob down, the husks remained at my feet
waiting to be swept up. There was no one else to do it.
I had driven everyone else away.
The broom was rubbed on one side to the nub
from the imbalance of my imperfect cleaning,
but the floor would thank me for it if it could.
Who would I thank? Why can't I remember
to keep my feelings more in balance than my cleaning?

Reaching Us

Breathing first starlight is the same
as a white peach stone, knife
edge on whet stone to hone it
to match the skills it will need,
is the same as
blue irises,
the harmonics of the green apple
in the yellow room,
the loom of light and the shadow
woven by the spider, is the same as
impaired vision, loss of smell,
the caged vocabulary releasing itself ---
that which goes beyond hesitation
is that which searches like pelican
trying to fill itself bill in an depleted area.
Things may take a thousand years to reach us;
but they do with clarity.

Letting Anger Go

Your mind is troubled, a broken hornet's nest.
Trees bring their lips
close to the long ago winds.
You bring a basket of sorrow.
The slowest brook is stillness moving.
It is the temperature of a wing in air-draft.
Hornets are in your heart.

Concentrate your mind through the eye of a needle.

Peace is a lavish tapestry of singing.
The stars are just beginning.
Cherry blossoms fall at your feet.

A.J. Huffman

A.J. Huffman is a poet and freelance writer in Daytona Beach, Florida. She has previously published her work in literary journals, in the U.K. as well as America, such as Avon Literary Intelligencer, Eastern Rainbow, Medicinal Purposes Literary Review, The Intercultural Writer's Review, Icon, Writer's Gazette, and The Penwood Review. Find A.J. Huffman, and additional information and links to her work at http://www.facebook.com/profile.php?id=100000191382454

Unaligned. In a Forgotten Wind. (Featured Poem)

At night
she could see the window.
Shining red.
And webbed like blood.

But the cord
around her neck
was too tight
to be a dream.
And pulled her back
over the bars.
Until she melted.
And bent
with his every command.

Dancing in the Temple of Hell

The music
of the moon
shatters
inside the vein.
Like a dream
left
to burn
between the arms
of a sun.

Implosion

The line touched me.
With its bloody eye.
Focused.
And unforgiving
in its beauty.

It entered me.
A welcome lover.
Baring me
in its breath.
A mouth.
Filled with exquisite pain.
And a cold heat
singing.
My requiem.
In B flat.

Its blue brilliance
was pure death.
All sexy seduction.
Calling.
And I followed.
The levels.
Crashing.
Through the spectrum.

Burning.
From my fingers.
Until I was gone.

Post Card

Not like this.
Not while the smell of piss and shit
lays in gutters and alleys.
Now while these bed sheets reek of sweat,
and not while the front door
hangs open after you left.
No, you sonova bitch: not like this.

But thanks very much
for the twenty you left on the table,
you cheap bastard.
That'll get me coffee and a bagel
and maybe, if I'm lucky,
a cot with a clean sheet, blanket,
and no bugs to crawl over me tonight if:
If I can sleep through the grunts and groans
of five-minute specials in the other rooms.
If there's a light in the hallway.

I knew it would end sometime,
but don't worry:
I'll be all right.
I know where I'm going

(previously published online)

Driving Into November *(Featured Poem)*

October's colors fall
like so many broken promises.
Trees in the hills stand unclothed,
scarred and cut, riven by storms.
And I'm driving tonight
into November.

This road I've traveled before
into April's false spring,
June's summer solstice,
and August's dog days.
Now, this November night,
I drive between seasons—
harvest home,
gifts unthought of.
Hillside houselights few,
long spaces between
like empty inches on a map,
white where only words unspoken live,
ones you consider
yet make you slide your eyes away
from what you don't want to see.

Pieces of a Life Between Latitudes

1.

Each day I listen to show tunes.
I live lives of love found and lost,
Trespasses without forgiveness,
reconciliation without grace.
Rain upon the roof never enough
to drown consequences.

2.

Plaque strangled my father's brain.
He did not, could not, read.
He turned pages as if looking
for someone, someone,
to tell him my name.

3.

Lover, who's that on the phone?
Why do you turn away and lower your voice?
Do you use "Yes" and "No" in code?
Forsythia and lilac branches crisscross
like friends who search for sun,
but, not finding it,
turn upon themselves.

4.

I live between middle and northern latitudes:
seven pills at breakfast,
five at lunch,
one before bed.
Fitness experts never seem to age,
do they.

5.

Even as clouds reveal and hide the sun
trees shadow the ground:
ancestors who remember the Past
and what it teaches
so that we understand the Future.

Last Shot

Maybe you'll answer this,
maybe not.
If you do,
if we meet,
you probably won't meet me again.
Most women don't.
Why?
I'm out of touch with things.
Out of time.
How old am I?
I remember Nam.
Height?
I can reach the top shelf at the supermarket.
Weight?
I wear the same clothes I wore five years ago.
Married?
Divorced.
Kids?
Two: I see them once, maybe twice a year.
Other?
I don't go to clubs,
I don't hang out.
Been through that—
all the noise,
the used word play,
verbal foreplay...
Nothing in it,
except tired and sorry silence
of the next morning.
I don't go to church,
don't go to movies:
same old, same old.
What do I do?
I read about the Past.
Where do I like to go?
Someplace where I'm the only human
as far as I can see.

What can I offer?
If you've read this far,
if you've listened,
if you're still interested, you already know.

Old Friends Then and Now

They appear to me when I read the paper
drink a beer or drive long distance.
We never shared a table,
but we're old friends.

Kay hung out at the Derby Inn
and offered confessions to Jim Beam
and Gentleman Jack.

Clarence was always first in line
but last to enter the Broadway Theater
at Saturday matinees.

Charlie, Curt, and Patty gave their lives in Nam,
supposedly to help create Democracy
and stop the spread of Communism.
They never learned the truth
about the Gulf of Tonkin incident,
back-door deals, and presidential papers.

Every town has them:
so-called weirdos who suddenly invoke the heavens
or some strange power
only they believe in.
Their lives end too early.
Forgotten flowers wither under summer sun.
Winter rain freezes carved names
and dates.

Dead now, old friends still speak.
They still matter.
They always will.

Somewhere In The Night.

No bank accepts this currency,
the exchange-rate is unfavorable,
and this poet won't pay the fee, anyways.

The currency I carry is 'time'...
it's childhood and youth...
paths leading here and there,
and in particular, nowhere;

it's travels I've been on,
and now,
ready to invest my savings,
bankers look at me with blank stares,
and tellers tells me to go elsewhere.

No credit-card pays expenses...
no ATM accepts.

I walk the streets,
backpack and sleeping-bag for comfort.

Outside town I find a lovely, secluded place
amidst trees, flowers, and scents,
a bird's evening-song,
and memories carried by a clear spring.

I pitch my tent,
and start a fire for the evening.

I write in its warm glow.

The past comes for a visit, yet again,
to ask in a poem why things are like this,
to tell me I'm rich as I drink my last coffee,
tear up old photographs,
and letters from a woman who should've known better.

Events are finding their resting place;
personal fate and story deposit their strange currency.

Tomorrow...yes...perhaps tomorrow
I'll find a place to store my sleeping-bag.

Autumn is approaching.

Tomorrow...yes...perhaps tomorrow.

Refugee.

"An exit permit is required to travel where you wish to go"

I was told

"and we don't see your name registered.

You're not a subject of this poetic realm,
and the process of application usually takes about six months.

If you'll please fill out this form, in triplicates,
I'll stamp it for further processing."

'Six months, you say?...!...
but I can't wait that long;
my family is waiting on the other side,
and I'm desperate, I tell you!'

"Sorry, Sir,
but procedure has to be followed,
even in war-time.

So many refugees come through here,
and we only have berth for a few at a time."

I return to my rented room, mind in a haze,
not knowing what to do.

There's a knock on my door.

It's the telegram-boy with a message.

I take it, and pay him a tip.

I close and lock the door,
pour myself a drink,
light my pipe,
and read:

"Hello, darling.

If these words reach you,
I know I'll never see you again.
The kids are fine, and miss you very much."

I fold the telegram.

Love is cut short, when two worlds collide.

I walk about in my room, talking to myself,
talking to my wife and my kids...
talking words to imagine being there

as while the gramophone-needle
slows down on music only I can hear.

Tomorrow Is Another Day.

10:45 PM.

After a long shift serving the obese,
the fast-food-worker bicycles home
through the dark, almost-deserted streets;

he is heading for his down-town-rented room,
where awaits the all-in-one micro-wave tv-dinner,
the lottery-ticket of "not a winner",
a bed with not-so-clean sheets,
loneliness of another night
without love or promises,
and/but
"tomorrow is another day."

Frank De Canio

Frank De Canio has been published in over 200 magazines (and/or e-zines); Danger, Pleiades, Genie, Write On!!, Red Owl, Nuthouse, Love's Chance, Words of Wisdom, Rook publishing, Illogical Muse, Writer's Journal, The Lyric, Free Lunch, Art Times, Pearl; Hazmat, Medicinal Purposes, Blue Unicorn and Ship of Fools, Raintown Review, and others pending. On the web he's on POETZ, Contemporary Rhyme, Language and Culture, and Thick with Conviction.

Shifty as Charged

The springtime peppers holes in my conceit.
For memory is masked in woolen clothes
at winter when I trudged through snow and sleet.
I still insist on fancy's youthful pose
when there are few infractions to recall
that aren't cloaked in muffling masquerade.
But bare-all spring commemorates with gall
the life of each post-mortem escapade,
like crimes ticked off from my contested years.
And how can I ignore a rap sheet flung
accusingly with evidence from peers
who many years before this charge I'd hung
around with. Hostile witnesses to age,
they seal Time's verdict at the judgment stage.

Clockwise

I owe it to myself to be on time
or not accept its challenge to compete.
Since celebrated as a paradigm
of knighthood, I won't grumble in defeat.
Nor will I implement my whip and spurs
to keep my hurtling charger on its course
until the inevitable occurs,
with shameful tumbles, and a voice that's hoarse.
I won't besiege Time's chariot in flight,
as though I were a coward in reverse
by tilting at a windmill that can't fight.
For reeling in its aftermath is worse.
So either I'm positioned for the fray
or bide my time, lest there be grief to pay.

TSB/86 ~ ARTWORK / *Rex Sexton* ~ Witch

~ ~ ~

The Pumpkin
Fiction by Ron Koppelberger

Restoring the shattered remnants of the pumpkin would be difficult. Crew Frisk Took a long narrow piece of solder from the roll and heated it with acetylene torch. The Pumpkin was a tarnished tin and it had been smashed and broken by some of the local hoodlums. He heated the surface of the first edge and smeared the melting solder into place careful to connect the seams of the two edges. The pumpkin smiled in half at Crew as he turned it in his gloved hands. A bright orange light lit his living room and he sighed with the ghosts of a thousand Halloweens. The solder slid easily across the next piece as the metal glowed red, almost too hot for the solder. He blew on the tin and it cooled rapidly accepting the new seam.

The last piece was the top, but first.........but first. He went to the body on the living room floor and re-moved one of it's eyes, plop and squish as he pushed it into the tin pumpkin. "Very nice!" he whispered as he licked the blood from his sticky fingers, "Very nice indeed!" The pumpkin was almost complete. He fixed the final seam with the solder and torch as the eye looked from within the confines of the tin pumpkin.
He finished and took the pumpkin to the front porch with the others, a long row of metal pumpkins all soldered and fixed with the stares of all the local hoodlums and trespassers. He giggled and lit a candle, the first trick or treaters would be arriving soon and he had a surprise for them.

An hour later the doorbell rang and he raced to answer it, "Trick or Treat!" they sang on the other side of the door. He grabbed the bowl and opened the door.
The trick or treaters staggered backward and screamed as he pushed the bowl toward them; it was full of the fingers and toes of the hoodlums. The children ran away screaming as he laughed after them.

Crew Frisk made the news the next day and as they lead him away he waved at the cameras and pointed to his eyes, there were bandages there and empty eye sockets beneath. "I'll be seeing ya!" he laughed as the police pushed him into the back of a patrol car. They would discover the tin pumpkins secret weeks later after the first winter snows and the end of fall.

~ ~ ~

Far From It
Fiction by Ron Koppelberger

He was founded in dark acclaim and consort with the shadows of vile trifle and trashy value. He curtailed courtesy for disinterested regard, Peevish illusory spells of cold contemplation. Kyote Yellow was sure in his impulsive berries, berries rich red and full o blood he thought, "Ripe fer tha pickin." he said aloud.

Kyote was an airless gasp of heat on a sunny day, kept undeviating, dire in aggressive mockery for the hungry beast, the concrete silhouette of a city in motion. Kyote turned the radio dial to its loudest,

"Disorder, carnivore

Disorder carnivore,

In my nonchalant hue

An adept invulnerable rue,

And a condition of hate

In my second rate,

Disorder and bane,

Complexity, insane,

Disorder and rain......

In buckets and barrels cups and chalices

Of cool disorder baby,

Disorder."

Kyote yelled to the empty street, "Disorder, YEEEEEEEEEHHHHHHHHHAAAAAAAAAAA!" Kyote

walked the voyage of secret shifting anger and charcoal burnt escape, looking for his prey, his mark,

his lump of clay to mold and tenant.

Kyote glanced across Vermillion Boulevard and paused. Two tall muscle bound black hearts in

salvo. An ancient woman rolling a shopping cart full of tin cans. They were harassing her,

yelling and shoving her between each other. She cringed and fell to the concrete sidewalk. The

two burst out with whoops and screams of conquest as they yanked her purse free from her

grasp. Kyote remained motionless in a fascinated paralysis. One of the men pumped his fist in

the air toward kyote as he ran back down vermillion boulevard. Kyote smirked and ignored him

as he continued his voyage. "Takin a ticket o leave." he sang "I'm far from it."

Ron is a poet, a short story writer and an artist. He has written 103 books of poetry over the past several years and 18 novels. He is always looking for an audience. He has published 700 poems, 723 short stories and 190 pieces of art in over 293 periodicals, books, anthologies and 11 radio Broadcasts. He has been published in England, Australia, Canada, Japan, India, Mauritius, Italy, France, Germany, China, Spain and Thailand. He has been Published in The Stray Branch, The Fringe, Write On!!! (Poetry Magazette) Static Movement, Necrology Shorts and Record Magazine. He is a member of The Poet's society, The Fiction Guild as well as The Isles Poetry Association and The Dark Fiction Guild. His art is viewable on Facebook under will806095@bellsouth.net.

Website- Ronniewk.Weebly.com (Swamplit)
Website- Shadowsatnighttide.weebly.com
Website- Wolffray.blogspot.com
Website- Ravenswont.blogspot.com
Website- E-zine Ethrealsouls.blogspot.com
Website- E-zine Fathermostdream.blogspot.com
Website- Mirageinblame.blogspot.com
Website- Horrorrush.blogspot.com
Website- Ravensbloodpoetry.weebly.com
Website- Abutterflywhisperspoetry.weebly.com
Website- Snakefuss.blogspot.com
Wolffray.proboards.com

Daniel J. Langton

Daniel J. Langton's work has appeared in Poetry, the Paris Review, the Atlantic Monthly, the Iowa Review, the TLS and similar publications. His QUERENCIA won the Devins Award and the London Prize. His SELECTED POEMS will appear this year.

AGAIN   THIS   EVENING

There are those who say, "I'll never forget"

when they just remembered, smiling over

the highball glass, tapping their cigarette.

When that happens I am in the Rover

with you in Palisades Park, my head down,

looking at your legs, the moon pretending

it has nothing better to do, the clown

on the dashboard nodding at the ending.

You have two children.   I know you know that,

I am telling the poem.   The rest is gone,

the Rover smashed, I moved away.   And yet.

You are what I see, those stockings, that hat,

When someone I am with goes on and on,

Their eyes slowing down,   "I'll never forget."

Krikor Der Hohannesian

Krikor Der Hohannesian lives in Medford, MA. His poems have appeared in many literary journals including The Evansville Review, The South Carolina Review, Atlanta Review, Louisiana Literature, Hawai'i Pacific Review and Connecticut Review. His first chapbook, "Ghosts and Whispers", was published by Finishing Line Press (2010) and was nominated for the Pen New England and Mass Book Awards. A second chapbook, "Refuge in the Shadows", is forthcoming from Cervena Barva Press. He serves as Assistant Treasurer of the New England Poetry Club.

A WAY OF LIFE

Great clattering outside
the bedroom window, early morning
a late January day – dissonance of demolition,
splintering pine boards, screech of metal on metal,
ripping of upholstery. A frayed hassock pitches
from the second story sun porch, throaty
metallic reverberations thud
the steel bottom of the trash trailer.
A cane-backed chair, a wicker hamper,
cheap-jack panel...a roustabout, black-stubbled,
says the house has been sold.

Henry and his wife both near 100 years,
eight decades together in this his house of birth,
defying entropy – suddenly vanished
like wraiths in the night.

So little I knew about them, she hanging out
a second floor window reeling in the weekly
laundry in the heat of summer and chill
of winter, sheets starchy white – how fresh
they must have smelled!

He, deaf as granite and not much for small talk,
eight years and we had spoken once- about
cutting down the Norway next to the chain-link,
more sunlight for the tomatoes and broccoli. "Oh,
fine by me," he allowed and went on
scruffing up yellowed thatch.

                    Now a bare bulb glows

a lone beacon in the attic window. The clothesline,
unburdened, flaps in the icy March wind. A blue
silence stares blankly from across the back fence.

WHAT DO YOU DO?

Armenian grief is a fathomless, boundless sea
-Hovannes Toumanian (1903)

What do you do
   with the ghosts of melancholy
      that lurked in dark, dusty niches?

What do you do
   with lies that lay hidden
      like a smoldering peat bog?

What do you do
   with a thirst for what was lost
      hanging like beads of fog on the skin?

What do you do
   with the weight of the unspeakable,
      the grief which you could not lift?

These tears I shed,
   that fall on your headstones
      under the weeping willow,
         these tears are for you.

Catfish McDaris

Catfish McDaris. is a journeyman New Mexican bricklayer. He has been published widely for 20 years. His work has appeared in NYQ, Rattle, Louisiana Review, Chiron, Haight Ashbury, Pearl, Main St. Rag, Slipstream, & Cafe Review. His last big reads were in NYC & The Shakespeare & Co. Bookstore in Paris.

Climbing Icicles

I climb the icicles
while snowballs are
flung into my orb

My words dance across
the paper, each letter a
trained flea stepping in a
dab of paint

A nuance, shades &
shadows of emotion,
agony despair elation hope

Piano keys searching for
the melody that will pull
that secret string inside
my heart & yours.

Spaces Dreams

See billion specks
Of fast moving stars
On the edges
Speeding by clearly
Slowly slowing down
Upon a world or place
In a point unfathomable
Descriptions get lost
Once touched by rays
Human hand disappears
A dance of dreams
With unnamed galaxies

S Mail Received

Moving toward the proto-stars
View dust rings stringing like guitars
Journey onward day after day
Destination the Milky Way

Passing along cloud nebula
Competing with cluster gala
Take in sights from the cargo bay
Destination the Milky Way

Molecules perform helix wave
Message recorded sent to save
Signal received on S mail ray
Destination the Milky Way

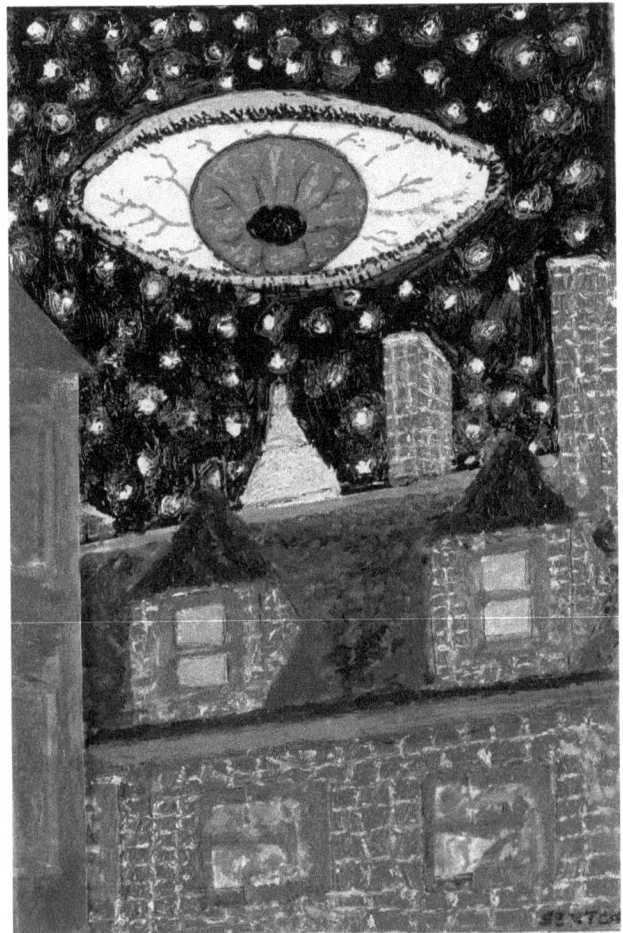

Artwork, *"Echoes in the Attic"* by Rex Sexton

Simon Perchik

Simon Perchik is an attorney whose poems have appeared in Partisan Review, The New Yorker and elsewhere. For more information, including his essay "Magic, Illusion and Other Realities" and a complete bibliography, please visit his website at www.simonperchik.com.

*

Again the sky rubbing against my legs
the way a dog closes its eyes
--I wade toward a place

that has your hairline, your nose
lips the same--tonight's no different
although these stars once side by side

behind their invisible starting line
--a few already clustered in the lead
some last and between I walk

from Gemini to Sirius to Orion
--all 14 miles by myself
and in my hands an empty glass

that magnifies the sky --I still look
for clues, for the ankles, the yes or no
as if the night has already forgotten

what is dead, what isn't, what
is hiding in the step by step
across an old footprint that might be there

might still be wandering and its bark
try once more for distance
the way a timekeeper's pistol is grasped

held up, but the stars
slip from under, drowning before my eyes
--the sun still alone, coming back

with yesterday, today, tomorrow
with the closed windows and the streets
left out too long.

*

This birthmark through my neck
expects these storms, waits
the way an iron rod pointing north
and in the darkness to volcanoes, water

--it learned to wake my jaws at night
for steam, drinking from the patch
and grunts pushed back into the cup
that always cracks

that must like this portable electric range
filled with crushed seawalls, tea leaves
lightning --one o'clock in the morning
--one eye at first, already thirsty

already drilling for water
for the still wanted spark
--cup after cup :a bridge higher, higher
and the sea that was born from these storms

that keeps looking under :waves
that let nothing pass, taste
from one arm holding another
attached to some invisible dog

still asleep, waiting under this table
as if a ladder
and soon more stars :missing pieces
melting this darkness for its thunder

its side to side through my throat
almost water again and my bare scar
as if it belongs
even without the stitches
the wires and craters.

James Dye

James Dye is an undergraduate at Northeast Iowa Community College. He'll be attending the University of Dubuque this fall to work on an english major and a minor in sociology. Since 2009 his poems and short stories have appeared in a number of publications including the Ampersand, Poor Mojo's Almanac(k), Aphelion, The Cynic Online Magazine, Strange, Weird, and Wonderful Magazine, cc&d magazine, The Clockwise Cat, O Sweet Flowery Roses, Scifaikuest, Dogzplot, Calliope Nerve, Shoots and Vines, Outshine, Pandora's Imagination, Mad Swirl, Moon Drenched Fables, Opium, Word Catalyst Magazine, Sorcerous Signals, Cats with Thumbs, (A Brilliant) Record Magazine, Sorean Gothic Magazine, A Generation Defining Itself Volume 8, Midwest Literary Magazine, and many more. You may download his free poetry e-book at www.poemhunter.com or visit his blog atwww.jamesjdye.blogspot.com

Vein of Taunt

Now we see in a dim-mirror, darkly,
a riddle but then face to face.
Partial, yet, fully known-eternity.
A broken reflection of the truth
clear and polished like a simile.
Darkon scatterer uncertainly derived.
The ancient hands of language touch
alluding nothingness, the wicked walk.

Meaningless Heart

The sun sets. Silence is heard. I'm
Wet, filled with pain. It never dries.
The Judgment on my soul is mine,
as deep as the ocean goes, through.
I cannot sleep, I spill wine and type
of mysterious cheese and cliché tripe,
on this drug, poetry, the abyss of infinity.
A trapdoor to my soul, in the sand, that
river dripping down slowly from my lips,
searching, for commas, to remove the,
trapped between spaces. I'm worn out.
My heart, has no meaning, what a crime.

Poor Cousin Ed

Ed is a genius.
Bumbling and balding,
He signs his name Ed 67'
So people know it's him and not his father.

We didn't know where he was for fifteen years
Because we didn't understand
His autism or whatever it was.

He's got these crazy theories too.
I saw him last at a wedding in the parking lot arranging bottles in a big V.

I get e-mails.
I heard he took off
In a car looking for rain.

Jay Dardes

Jay Dardes is a retired psychotherapist who lives in the woods of northwest Pennsylvania with his wife, Elaine, and dog, Gretel.

Omen

Even in your sleep

you pull away from

my slightest touch.

Artwork, *"Talking Heads"* by Rex Sexton

Pat

You said we had lost our freedom,

Locked in our bond of commitment.

Well, now I'm a free man, my friends,

Subject only to misery.

My Dad's Way

So it's happened again. We aren't speaking. The first time
it was the circumstances of divorce, a mother's fear
that you would take me away; not your choice, but a boy
couldn't know that. The second time, it was over religion.
A good reason if world history is an indicator,
but I don't want to talk about that. But when you said
just before you kicked me out that I would need you one day,
grovel back, asking for help but that you wouldn't be there
for me, I thought – before the third fateful disowning –
that those were old, regretfully cruel, hasty words.
All these years (has it really been a decade?) I've declared you
a monster for fulfilling your prophecy – and other things:
you know how you are, how you intentionally like to be annoying
by singing at people who you supposedly love
instead of talking to them; and your unaccountable anger
that everyone in the family fears will result in violence,
and sometimes did. But now I realize, just today,
how insecure you are, how far from extremely strong,
to the point of often belittling others to feel better
about your so-called manhood. Who hurt you, father?
I don't guess I'll ever know. But I've learned to pity you
instead of hate you, hate you for abandoning me
when I couldn't work, and asked for (needed) your help.
Money was not your problem; it was fear. How shameful
to have a mentally ill son. How easy to deny
if you couldn't see me. Could such things be hereditary,
as the doctors say? And I'm the fool who misses you.

Featured ⬚⬚⬚ Poet
G David Schwartz

Fall/Winter 2013

G. David Schwartz - the former president of Seedhouse, the online interfaith committee. Schwartz is the author of A Jewish Appraisal of Dialogue and Midrash and Working Out Of The Book Currently a volunteer at The Cincinnati J, Schwartz continues to write. His newest book, Shards And Verse (Baltimore, PublishAmerica, 2012) is now in stores or can be order on line.

Names are not real people, in my work.

DavidSchwartzG@AOL.Com

Without Wings Made Me Tear

Without wings made me tear
Made me wish that you were here
I would let you borrow do
My absence of wings so true
Without wings made me seem
To be a burred bird
and as I feel my wet eyes drupe
Its just the drupe drop of words
I lay my eyes beneath with cries
And end up with only sighs
And being thus so wingless
I pound my fists upon my chest

They Hit Me Like A Pillow

I sat down at a committable conformable desk
I had earlier cleared the mess
then I let my eyes drop onto her verse
Wide awake in a flash
   Some people, so I hear
   think beauty is a body
   some believe it is a part
   But I have studied Aristotle
   And althought I've forgot
I seem to see some beauty
On the printed page
Which makes be cry
Or makes be go in rage
   But with her, without her here
   I thought a bit about her ear
   And wondered where I could go to hear
   Those gentle droppings of a tear
A wise sage one day said
"Beauty's only shin deep
But the more I read these lines I find
You do need skin for beauty
   And there they were
   The trouble-less laughter lines
   Which with the warm days
   Still bring good surprise
And like a pillow they hit me
All stones flew to let me be

Erren Geraud Kelly

Erren Geraud Kelly is a poet based in New York City, by way of Louisiana, by way of Maine, by way of California and so on. Erren has been writing for 21 years and has over three dozen publications in print and online in such publications as Hiram Poetry Review, Mudfish, Poetry Magazine(online) and other publications. Erren's most recent publication was in " In Our Own Words," a Generation X poetry anthology; Erren was also published in other anthologies such as " Fertile Ground," Beyond The Frontier " and other anthologies. Erren recieved a B.A. in English-Creative Writing from Louisiana State University in Baton Rouge. Erren also loves to read andloves to travel, having visited 45 states and Canada andEurope. The themes in Erren's writings vary, but Erren has always had a soft spot for subjects and people who are not in the mainstream. But Erren never limits themself to anything, and always tries to keep an open mind.

JOSHUA (aubade)

fingers his saxophone
like the buttons on
the back of a woman's
dress
if jazz is the soul of the blues
it lives in his dark eyes
his father's warrior spirit
is in his walk
grandfather's eyes
watches over him
every morning
as it rises in the
dawn

www.ingramcontent.com/pod-product-compliance
Lightning Source LLC
Chambersburg PA
CBHW081633040426
42449CB00014B/3291